**A Director's Guide**

# Partnerships with people

BUSINESS PERFORMANCE THROUGH YOUR PEOPLE

*Editor, Director Publications:* Tom Nash
*Managing Editor:* Lesley Shutte
*Production Manager:* Victoria Davies
*Head of Business Development and Sponsorship:* Simon Seward
*Design:* Halo Design
*Chairman:* Tim Melville-Ross
*Managing Director:* Andrew Main Wilson

Published for the Institute of Directors
by Director Publications Ltd
Institute of Directors, 116 Pall Mall
London SW1Y 5ED

*Editorial:* 0171 766 8910
*Sponsorship:* 0171 766 8833
*Production:* 0171 766 8960
*Facsimile:* 0171 766 8990

Printed in England

# YOURS TO HAVE AND TO HOLD
## BUT NOT TO COPY

Director Publications
116 Pall Mall
London SW1Y 5ED

Kogan Page Ltd
120 Pentonville Road
London N1 9JN

© Director Publications 1998

British Library Cataloguing in Publication Data
A CIP record for this book is available from the British Library
ISBN 0 7494 2830 9

Printed and bound in Great Britain by St Ives plc

# Contents

# Putting your people first

## Tim Melville-Ross, Director General, Institute of Directors

The title of this Director's Guide contains two of the key words in business today. The first, partnerships, is vital because companies are more dependent than ever on a complex web of mutually beneficial partnerships – with advisers, suppliers, customers, shareholders, and, of course, with employees.

The second, people, is crucial because thankfully – in most businesses anyway – employees are no longer regarded merely as units of production or as costs. They are human beings with knowledge, skills and, above all, feelings! Employees will not be motivated – or even retained – if their needs and aspirations are not recognised, if they are not properly led, informed and involved in the enterprise and appraised and rewarded for their contribution to it.

It may seem obvious that businesses' partnership with people is crucial to their success, but it is surprising how often companies fail to nurture that relationship. The responsibility for doing so lies squarely on directors.

If directors think of their employees as resources, to be used when required, and discarded, downsized or re-engineered when times get tough, then the chances are that those employees will treat their company – and its customers – in the same uncaring manner. On the positive side, however, if directors actually live up to one of their most overworked phrases and really do treat their people as their "greatest asset" they will be amazed at the loyalty, enthusiasm, innovation and productivity they will get back in return.

# Getting out of the Stone Age

## Julian Richer, Chairman, Richer Sounds

We are nearly in the 21st century and most employers are still in the Stone Age. No matter how many books they have read and how much technology they have bought, the directors of many organisations in this country are primitive in their understanding of the most important part of their business – the people.

The most important – and usually the most neglected – people in any business are the employees. And the most important and neglected employees are those who actually deal with the customer. Time and again, I've found if a business has problems with customer service, it comes back to how that company treats its staff. The lesson everywhere is the same – focus on people so that they are motivated and productive and, in turn, treat your customers well.

To improve the performance of your people, you first have to ask yourself if managers and staff are working within a sound framework. Does your company have clear controls? Is everyone properly trained to do their job? Are people working to targets they understand and is their performance being continually measured? Secondly, are people motivated? Are they properly rewarded for their efforts? Is working for your organisation fun? The key to success is getting the right combination of control and motivation throughout your company.

We need to get out of the Stone Age, not only for the sake of business profits, but for the health of society too. This guide will help you do it.

# Chapter 1

# Partnerships with people

**Nigel Crouch, an industrialist with the DTI's Innovation Unit, highlights the findings of one of the most in-depth investigations of recent years into how successful and innovative organisations manage to bring the best out of their people to improve their business performance**

What does a major producer of chemicals have in common with a small spring manufacturer? Or a major retail company, with a small graphics company? The success of each of these businesses, and for that matter, all others, depends on their people.

Even a business which seemingly has everything going for it will not flourish if it lacks innovation. Making new ideas happen in every part of the organisation really is the key to winning with your customers. But it is only by involving every employee that companies can exploit all their innate strengths and respond to the ever more rigorous demands of the market. They are the richest source of innovation for any company.

## A PARTNERSHIP APPROACH

The *Partnerships with people* report itself embodies a strong partnership approach, having been produced by the DTI and DfEE, but with close involvement of the IoD and a large number of other partners. The report is based on hundreds and hundreds of interviews at all levels within companies over a two-year period and provides a wealth of practical insights from the organisations visited.

The participating companies represented a diverse range of sectors – their only common link being superior performance over time. was All agreed to share their financial performance data to

## PUTTING PEOPLE FIRST

- 90 per cent of those interviewed said that management of people had become a higher priority in the past three years.

- 90 per cent of companies have a formal training policy and plan – derived from the business plan.

- 97 per cent of interviewees thought that training was important or critical to the success of the business.

- 100 per cent of the organisations have a team structure.

- 65 per cent of companies with teams formally train their employees to work in teams – it doesn't just happen!

- 60 per cent of companies with teams formally train their team leaders so that the team systems become effective more quickly.

prove sustained success. The aim of the research was to determine how accomplished UK companies are at ensuring that every employee can have, and is seen to have, a role in the success of their workplace, by being allowed to contribute to their full potential to help improve overall business performance.

As a starting point we wanted to know how many companies could demonstrate that they valued their staff, and how many had at least begun to create a people-friendly working environment. Interviews and focus groups were conducted with people right across the business, from chief executives, managing directors and middle managers right through to the shop floor, where we found that perceptions often varied quite markedly depending on who we were talking to.

New ideas can be exploited anywhere within an organisation. At Leyland Trucks, operating costs have been reducing year-on-year due to improved efficiency drives suggested by employees. John Oliver, chief executive, comments: "The company has seen a 35-per-cent reduction in costs within two and a half years by improving quality. There are an average of 21 ideas per employee today. Compare this to 1990 when there were nil. Our people have accomplished this."

## IT'S BETTER TO MANAGE THAN BE MANAGED

Today's companies have fewer layers of management, with more responsibility deployed to individuals. Since the eighties, there has been a radical change in the structure of organisations brought about by the realisation that a company's primary focus needs to be its customers. Gone are the rigid, hierarchical boundaries separating workers from "the management". Instead many companies now operate networks of teams – the company as a whole being the main "team". As individual employees take on more responsibility, it is strong leadership that senior executives must provide. In this way, the best organisations manage themselves rather than being managed and are better able to respond to customer demand quickly and effectively.

It was interesting that, while there was unanimous agreement that the fundamental concepts behind empowerment were absolutely essential, the word itself was strongly disliked. It was often seen as management speak for downsizing or dumping and, if not implemented properly, could lead to chaos and anarchy. One managing director summed it up when he said: "We never use the word "empowerment". You can't empower people. You can only create the climate and structure where they will take responsibility."

## THE FIVE PATHS TO SUSTAINED SUCCESS

All the leading organisations that we visited really involved their people in where they were going and how they were getting there by following what is described in the report as the Five Paths to Sustained Success. These are:

- *Shared goals – understanding the business we are in;*

- *Shared culture – agreed values to bind us together;*

- *Shared learning – continuously improving ourselves;*

- *Shared effort – one business driven by flexible teams;*

- *Shared information – effective communication throughout the company.*

## SHARED GOALS

By genuinely sharing the planning of the business with as many of your people as possible, you are strengthening their commitment to the future of the business as well as ensuring that you get much more realistic plans. It is also the best way to ensure that the whole organisation knows where it is going and what its goals are. Admittedly, this approach takes time and requires a degree of courage but, as an employee at one company pointed out: "It is not the sole prerogative of senior managers to come up with the good ideas."

## SHARED CULTURE

An organisation's culture is the sum total of its employees' inherited ideas, beliefs, values and knowledge. Cultures can be shaped and, indeed, most successful companies have this as part of their strategy. But a company's culture must be managed to ensure that everyone understands its values with respect to its people, its customers, its suppliers and to the wider community in which it operates.

A sound culture is a very powerful force within any organisation. Challenges to the company from outside are met in an atmosphere of co-operation and conciliation, with everyone seeking to add to the solutions of the problems. But a word of warning: cultures are extremely fragile. Months and even years of trust and mutual respect can be destroyed overnight if a lack of respect and inequalities are perceived. You have to "walk the talk."

## SHARED LEARNING

The importance of shared learning cannot be over-stated. An unskilled, unwilling, unresponsive workforce can undermine and negate even the best corporate strategies.

So, once a company has its goals and plans in place, it needs to assess the existing skills of all employees to determine what further learning and training will be required if both the company and the individual are to realise their full potential. As the workforce becomes more skilled, the visions of the company can become more ambitious because the full potential of the people is released into an environment of achievement. Getting the level of "stretch" right is crucial: too much will only cause stress and too little will lead to boredom.

## SHARED EFFORT

The people we spoke to invariably enjoyed working in teams and were therefore more highly motivated. However, teams will only be effective if they are properly structured and individuals are trained in teamworking. Care must be taken to ensure that teams do not compete with one another in a counter-productive way and that the flow of information from and to teams is reliable and constructive. Good teamworking provides the building blocks for the organisation to integrate effort and solve problems.

## SHARED INFORMATION

Change in a company is managed through the efficient exchange of information and ideas. Many companies work hard at downward communication, but in order to be most effective, information exchange needs to take place up, down and across the whole organisation. Many companies have discovered the value of open communications – telling the truth at all times without undue optimism or pessimism – and of establishing an informal atmosphere, with bureaucracy and meetings kept to a minimum.

## THREE STAGES OF DEVELOPMENT

Another important factor to emerge from the research was that achieving a true "people partnership" takes a long time and is no easy ride. We believe that it breaks down into three distinct stages within each of the five paths, at which certain elements of good practice must be established before the company moves forward to break new ground. These are:

- *Starting out*

- *Moving forward*

- *New horizons*

## KEY MESSAGES

Motivated, well-trained people are essential to the smooth running of any enterprise. It is only by engaging the aspirations and commitment of all employees that a business will be able to meet the needs of its customers effectively. However, there is no point in trying to impose the right values, culture, training or information on your employees. The only way to release your people's creativity and innovation is to show them that you trust them, and to give them responsibility within a clearly defined framework.

The companies that have embraced this new way of working, building strong relationships with their employees, are committed to the ideals of their partnerships.

Although some are at different stages of achievement than others, all agree that there is no other way forward. Each company must assess its own individual culture and build on those shared values and goals. But the closer that these goals represent the true aspirations of all the people in the organisation, the more likely it is that those goals will be achieved.

When "people partnerships" are really working, it hits you immediately – its the way you are greeted at reception, the whole atmosphere as you walk around.

It's friendly and fun, but there is also a high degree of stretch and a lot of challenges. The most striking feature is that there is a tremendous buzz everywhere, a real electricity in the air and it is an exciting place to be in... what also helps, of course, is that company performance is outstanding and, as we all know: success breeds success.

*How does your organisation rate on "people partnerships"? Turn to page 76 to work through the Partnerships with People questionnaire and checklist. Copies of the* Partnerships with people *report can be obtained free by telephoning the orderline number on page 79.*

# Chapter 2

# Is your brand image people-based?

**John Stevens, director of professional policy, the Institute of Personnel and Development, emphasises that a company's image is created by the entire workforce – not just the marketing department**

The question, "Is your brand image people-based?" is a difficult one to answer, but that does not mean that it will simply go away. Managers face a similar question about their organisation's strategy for the future. But, whereas a few years ago many organisations could simply ignore the people question (and even ignore the strategy question), the evidence is piling up that success – if not survival – depends on getting the answer right.

Organisations in different markets follow a wide range of product and service strategies. However, a basic division is between those organisations that want the vast majority of their people to work in a semi-mechanical way, following rules and with relatively little discretion, and those that base their success on people at all levels – using their initiative to add value in the eyes of the customer.

## SO WHAT MAKES THE DIFFERENCE?

The difference does not have to do with skill levels or with training spend, but with product and process differentiation, and with the ability to respond flexibly to the needs of both individual customers and the wider market. It has to do with what marketing people call "brand". At all levels, the difference between the organisations which have a brand based on the full contribution of their people and those which do not is becoming clearer.

On the one hand, there are companies that encourage employees to care and to innovate – to upgrade a passenger here, to sort out an urgent order there, to feed back an important piece of sales data – within acceptable parameters. On the other hand are those organisations which seek only to control – Esther Rantzen's "job's worth" organisations and others which under-utilise the opportunities for people to add value or influence customers by extending their judgement or skills.

### LEAVING BRAINS AT HOME

It is not that one approach is always better than the other. If a t-shirt is a t-shirt, just like any other t-shirt, and neither the product nor the organisation that produces it has a brand image, then robots will be as effective, though not necessarily as cheap as people. Organisations like this do not require their employees to bring their brain with them to work. Indeed, people may even get in the way.

However, organisations that can operate in this way are becoming ever more rare. People fulfil the role as an organisation's most important asset more clearly when they are required to use their ingenuity for positive customer-related purposes. And people at all levels are aware of this, as exemplified by this comment from a shopfloor worker making nuts and bolts: "The key to success is getting the right product to the right customer, on time, to a specific quality standard and being ready to adjust the order at a minute's notice."

It is clear that the product of this organisation has moved on. It is no longer an indistinguishable commodity; it has actually acquired its own brand, one based on the extended contribution of its people. And the brand does not depend solely on those employees who have obvious links with customers. The security man answering out-of-hours calls may have a more direct influence on customer relations than the managing director. Having people "on song" with the brand is important at all times. A sale, or the reputation of the brand, may be gained or lost in a moment of employee exasperation or inattention. These are the "static" arguments for a much more sophisticated approach to the management and development of people. There is also a "dynamic" argument. We all know that the organisation which innovates is more likely to get into more profitable markets and is likely to be more robust because its people are more attuned to the need for flexibility and change.

Yet, for many organisations the management of change is a source of frustration rather than strength. Getting staffing levels right is essential and relatively easy, but driving through changes in work and attitudes is still an up-hill battle. The culture of organisations, firmly rooted in "do as you are told", rather than "make your own decision and we will support you", needs to change. Changing culture is the most complex management task. And the development of an organisation's brand image will depend on its culture. It is the product of the whole firm and not just its marketing department or top management team.

Willingness to embrace change is still elusive. The willing contribution of employees, including managers, working with colleagues day to day, or working with their immediate boss, somehow evaporates and is replaced by suspicion and filibuster when larger scale and yet more important changes are on the horizon. The ingenuity of employees can all too easily be turned against the objectives espoused by the top management team and people emerge as the weak link in the chain. "This organisation would be all right if it wasn't for..."

## WHAT NEEDS TO BE DONE NOW?

For most organisations there are no easy answers but there are a few pointers. First, there is increasing evidence that the quality of people management does make a difference. Research evidence provided for the IPD by the Institute of Work Psychology at Sheffield University shows that for medium-sized manufacturing companies differences in people management policies and practices lie at the root of major differences in productivity and profitability improvement. The results, now widely publicised, have been thoroughly scrutinised. They show that people management practices explain much more of the variations over time in profitability between companies than practices which have previously been thought to be important, such as business strategy, emphasis on quality, use of advanced technology and investment in research and development.

Out of these, only research and development appears to be an important factor, but it explains much less of the performance differences between companies than people management. It is not that these other factors are unimportant, but that they are already treated seriously by most companies. In contrast, the researchers found that human resource management is one of the most neglected areas of managerial practice within organisations.

## DISTINGUISHING GOOD FROM BAD

The most important factors in the differences between the "good" and the "bad" relate to people management practices such as job design, flexibility and responsibility of shop floor jobs, the acquisition and development of skills and selection, induction, training and appraisal.

However, the most telling research results, as is often the case, relate to the comments of some of those interviewed. Some managers interviewed dismissed people management practices as "being relevant to larger companies". Others had every intention of "dealing with people issues when business issues had been effectively dealt with". The report concluded that: "For most, the rhetoric of employees being the most valuable resource was often simply rhetoric". It was only for a minority that human resource management and employee commitment, satisfaction and participation were central elements of their business strategy.

People management and development is often seen as a management task – rather than something that needs to be discussed by the board, and something which, beyond the annual pay round, can be left in the hands of line management and personnel. In a sense, it has to be. However, it is increasingly important that organisations work out what is wanted from their people and how they are going to go about this. They need to ask:

- *What are our organisation's people strengths and weaknesses?*

- *To what extent are these supporting or undermining its market objectives?*

- *How do we build a people-based strategy for the future?*

The top management teams of most organisations (the Sheffield study shows) do not even start to think in this way. And most of them lag behind in productivity and profitability. So the opportunity to put your organisation ahead is there. But changing to a people-based strategy is not easy. Quite apart from issues of attitude and understanding at the top team level – one major hurdle – there is the challenge of changing line management attitudes throughout the organisation. A five-to-ten-year strategy for organisational and cultural change in a tightly resourced business will require persistence and a great deal of professionalism as well as a shared vision.

### KNOW THYSELF

The change process has to start at the top. Knowing yourself is a key ingredient. Too many change processes fail because the chief executive or the top team have the vision but cannot see that what they are doing is incompatible with its implementation. They speak "new vision" and act "old vision".

As one director of group technology put it when asked how the companies were to be persuaded of the benefits of a new manufacturing systems approach: "We can't wait to persuade people, we have to drive it through". Sometimes thought and careful preparation has to take precedence over action and that is certainly true of the management of people. And as more and more organisations are finding out, people will them provide the payback.

# Chapter 3

# All in the mind

**Godfrey Golzen, editor Human Resources magazine, explains why everyone is talking about knowledge management**

When a US army unit in Bosnia encounters one of the marauding bands of irregulars that operate there, the officer in charge logs on to the Centre For Army Lessons Learned (CALL), a database in the US which contains visual images which might help him establish who they are, information on what patterns of behaviour he might expect from them and how any previous confrontations were dealt with.

Afterwards, the unit commander conducts an After Action Review in which he discusses with his men what happened, and the lessons that were learned. The results, and any new information that emerged, are then fed back into CALL, for future use by other units. Insight and experience are the added components that turn mere data into knowledge.

## TRANSFORMING HUMAN RESOURCE MANAGEMENT

Sharing knowledge and transferring it between the organisation and the individual in a continuous feedback loop is the essence of knowledge management, a concept which is transforming human resource management.

In recent years HR managers have been increasingly nervous about the way their position has been eroded by the automation of administrative processes and the move towards outsourcing key activities such as payroll administration, recruitment and training. While the phrase that "people are our great asset" regularly features in company reports, HR directors are a rarity in the boardroom of all but the largest companies. But if the real source of competitive advantage is in the people employed by a business, HR ought, by rights, to be taking up a strategic role at top levels. The discussion of how it can do so has generated more heat than light. Knowledge management looks like being the answer, which is why what the US army is doing has been closely watched by human resource gurus like Richard Pascale. He argues that its development into a more effective fighting force, since its disastrous intervention in Somalia a few years ago, has been based on its success in "knowing what it knows", and on the realisation that it is the people and how they apply the hardware that matter, not the hardware itself.

That is true of business as well. A report in US magazine *Strategy and Business* says that, since 1982, the value of various forms of knowledge in organisations has risen from 38 per cent of corporate assets to 80 per cent. Disturbingly, however, only 20 per cent of managers believed that it was being properly used.

## MEASURING KNOWLEDGE

Everyone knows it's there and that it's important. The problem, though, is that knowledge is hard stuff to measure and value by conventional means. However, Skandia a leading Swedish financial services firm, has aroused world-wide interest by its move to include intellectual capital – the gap between its market and book value – in its balance sheet.

Defining knowledge management and identifying what knowledge consists of in a business context has turned into a mini-industry of books, articles and conferences. Peter Murray, Research Fellow in Information Systems at Cranfield University, has produced as good a working definition of knowledge management as any:

> *"The collection of processes that govern the creation, dissemination and utilisation of knowledge to fulfil organisational objectives."*

Commentators such as Tom Stewart, author of *Intellectual Capital: The New Wealth of Organisations*, say knowledge in organisations has three components: human capital, customer capital and structural capital. Human capital is made up of the knowledge, experience and talents that people carry round in their heads and walk out with when they go home or leave. The reason why many acquisitions of knowledge-based companies fail is that the human capital leaks away.

## CUSTOMER CAPITAL

Customer capital, sometimes called relationship capital, is closely connected with it. It's the value of a firm's relationship with its customers and suppliers. When a firm's sales director leaves, for instance, a lot of its customer capital goes with him or her. Customer capital is increasingly important as the basis for extending a firm's activities, which is why retailers are interested in what people buy as much as in how much they spend.

Structural capital is the firm's products and brands, its unique selling points (USPs), the sources of its competitive advantage, its strategic alliances – all the stuff broadly lumped together under the term goodwill – as well as its management processes. "It is the transformation of human capital… into structural capital – the organisational capability that remains when your employees have gone home – that lies at the heart of management's new challenge," writes Elizabeth Lank.

This is both a technological and a human resources problem. Technologically there is a growing number of devices for capturing an organisation's knowledge:

- *Information storage in a way that can be easily accessed is being carried out by means of sophisticated document management and warehousing systems.*

- *Expertise directories, such as BT and Hewlett-Packard's electronic listings of internal know-how and know-who, make available names and contact details of subject matter experts – who knows what and where they are to be found.*

- *The use of communication tools such as videoconferencing, electronic bulletin boards, the Internet and intranet are vastly speeding up response times in a business environment where quick reaction is a source of competitive advantage.*

However, information technology only offers the instruments for sharing knowledge. The devil is in the implementation. Paradoxically, while people are an organisation's greatest asset, they are also liable to be the biggest obstacle here. One reason for that is insecurity – based on a fear of losing influence or control.

Another obstacle is that because knowledge is hard to measure, its importance is not accepted by management. Knowledge management programmes call for a big investment in technology as well as a change of mindset in which rewarding people for sharing knowledge becomes a significant factor in pay and promotion policies.

That in turn requires top management to identify and accept connections between knowledge and business strategy. For instance, if most of a company's profits are from products less than two years old, then sharing knowledge about new product development has a direct bearing on the firm's success.

## WHAT'S IN IT FOR ME?

But how do you get people to share their knowledge? "What's in it for me?" is often the open or implied question raised when they are asked to do so, especially now that the old employment bargain - job security in return for loyalty - has been replaced by the much tougher agenda of "a job for as long we need you".

Some of that question can be easily answered in money terms, by rewarding people not only for their knowledge and the value it adds, but also for the extent to which they are willing to share it. One of the leading Big Five accountancy and consultancy firms, Price Waterhouse Coopers, for instance, has re-engineered its reward and promotion policies by breaking away from its culture of "billable hours" – how much business managers bring in – and looking at how effective they are in sharing their knowledge with colleagues and subordinates.

Money is not the only factor, though. Nor should all the rewards go to the people who make the most visible contribution, though the number of millionaires among Microsoft's managers are a testimony of how well knowledge stars are doing. This has led, in some cases, to knowledge heavyweights being paid more than the managers for whom they supposedly work. But it is just as important to keep the people who hold the organisation together and who are the guardians of its structural knowledge, as it is to attract and retain the providers of human and relationship capital.

## WHERE'S THE MOTIVATION?

What turns knowledge workers on and motivates them to share their knowledge, particularly those with highly specialised skills, is not just money – and they may not even want promotion in the conventional sense.

What they are looking for are things like recognition inside and outside the organisation, courses which give them opportunities to develop their knowledge still further, funding for pet projects and maybe even the chance to work on their own ideas in company time, like 3M's famous "15 per cent rule" which encourages technical people to spend 15 per cent of their time on projects of their own choosing. As a result 25 per cent of the company's revenues comes from products introduced in the previous four years. Managing its knowledge base is a prime source of 3M's competitive advantage.

So is the people it hires. Many companies now recruit people not only for the skills they bring directly to the party, but also on whether they are prepared to share their knowledge with others and willing to take part in job rotation schemes that facilitate the transfer of expertise. The hard stuff of technology is, of course, inseparable from the softer aspects of knowledge management.

Research has shown that technofear, especially among older employees, is a further barrier to the transfer of knowledge. More people than is often realised need training in basic keyboard skills. Equally, fewer people are as comfortable with the use of the Internet and intranets as the publicity given to what are now key modes of communication might suggest.

Knowledge management is undoubtedly the current "hot ticket" in management discussion and just for this reason, it has attracted its sceptics. What, they say, is to distinguish it from previous fads like business process re-engineering?

The answer is that it relates directly to the speed with which IT is advancing and affecting the way business is conducted. It is, admittedly, uncharted territory, but it is signposted by familiar indicators – recruitment, retention, training, compensation and benefits and career paths. It is a road HR managers ought to be exploring. If they don't, Chief Knowledge Officers, a function that is beginning to appear in job ads, may step into their shoes.

**INVESTORS IN PEOPLE** *helped Waterfields Bakery reduce staff turnover by 44%. Call 0171 467 1900 to find out how.*

# Chapter 4

# Investing in people

As organisations change and develop, so must their people. Ian Luxford, marketing manager of Investors in People UK, discusses the role of the National Standard

The employers of almost a third of the UK workforce are now investing in their people. They are using the Investors in People National Standard as a practical tool to improve the organisation and its people continuously. This is because they realise that the crucial factor which determines the success of organisations is people.

Whatever the style of the organisation, what people are motivated to do – and can do consistently – gives their organisation the edge. People with the right knowledge, skills and attitudes to work ensure that, no matter what the business, its objectives are met. People are the real source of advantage.

Investors in People was a logical step from work done in the eighties on good practice in human resource development. Research carried out in the first half of the eighties showed how badly the UK was faring in training and skills development against its principal competitor countries. The challenges of change, new technology and competitiveness focused minds in business and government on the need to build the workforce for the nineties.

Investors in People was launched by the Secretary of State for Employment at the CBI Conference in November 1990. Three years later, the Department of Employment established a business-led company, Investors in People UK, to own, lead and manage the Investors in People Standard.

Over 10,000 UK organisations have now achieved the Standard and another 20,000 are formally committed to doing so. Farther afield, it has been adopted throughout Australia and is operating pilot projects in South America, New Zealand, Bermuda and parts of Europe. The practical nature of Investors in People and its foundation in good business sense has made it what it is today. Through its four principles, it addresses the people factors which make for success:

- Commitment
  *An Investor in People makes a commitment from the top to develop all employees to achieve its business objectives;*

- Planning
  *An Investor in People regularly reviews the needs and plans the training and development of all employees;*

- Action
  *An Investor in People takes action to train and develop individuals on recruitment and throughout their employment;*

- Evaluation
  *An Investor in People evaluates the investment and training and development to assess achievement and improve future effectiveness.*

Underpinning the four principles are 23 assessment indicators which serve as a permanent model for improvement that can take place continuously. The indicators specify the performance criteria to be satisfied. To achieve the Standard, an organisation must demonstrate to an independent assessor that its practices satisfy every indicator.

To become an Investor in People, it is essential that an organisation's top managers understand the Standard and its strategic implications for the organisation and its plans. A successful outcome will depend on top management commitment and support throughout the process:

- *Reviewing what is done currently against the requirements of the Standard to identify gaps. This may involve discussions with managers, staff and their workplace representatives, or the use of a survey covering some or all staff;*

■ *Developing an action plan to bridge the gaps, and planning to bring about necessary changes. Typically, this involves setting and resourcing objectives which align the skills of the people with the needs of the business;*

■ *Making the commitment to achieve the Standard and communicating that commitment to all staff: everyone in the organisation needs to understand their contribution to the grand plan;*

■ *Ensuring that the plan is put into practice throughout the organisation. Objectives are set for improving the knowledge, skills, attitude and performance of people, appropriate training and development action is taken and the results in improved job performance noted;*

■ *Putting forward the evidence to the external assessor showing that the Standard is met;*

■ *Assessment takes place, based on interviews with a representative sample of staff at all levels, and examination of relevant documents;*

■ *Following successful assessment, public recognition as an "Investor in People", feedback and planning for continuous development;* i.e. reward & recognition

■ *Continuous improvement, with people and systems moving forward as the needs of the organisation develop. To maintain the Standard, a company can choose between a full reassessment every three years, or an assessor's review every 12-15 months. This process can be facilitated through optional advisory services and membership of networks for groups of employers.*

Investors in People was developed by business, for business, so it has been designed not to create unnecessary paperwork. Three documents are required for assessment: the business plan; the training plan; and a training budget resource plan. Other documents produced in the normal course of business will be useful for assessment, but the process should not create a paperchase. Investors in People will work with what is done already – it is designed to be used in the most appropriate way for the organisation using it, and to complement that organisation's existing activities.

## PUTTING INVESTORS IN PEOPLE INTO CONTEXT

Hence, value will be added to work with other standards and models. For any standard to be achieved and to work effectively, everyone involved must know what it is for, why it is important and how it works. Many organisations have used Investors in People as a precursor to achieving externally-assessed quality, sector-specific, health and safety and environmental management standards. The Standard is highly complementary to the Business Excellence Model in that it represents an approach which fits all of the enabler criteria by being systematic, soundly based, requiring regular reviews and working best when fully integrated into normal business operations. Through evaluation, it also demonstrates a key link between its approach and the results which an organisation achieves.

Using the Investors in People Standard is essentially about enabling an organisation to achieve its objectives through the contributions of all its people. Organisations adopt the Standard for a variety of reasons. From research, the most commonly cited are "competitive edge", "framework for people management", "business/human resources alignment" and "benchmarking of training and development".

A recent detailed survey of over 230 Investors in People organisations found that customer expectations, competition, supply chain and cost pressures, new technology and environ-mental legislation all brought about change programmes which had their people/skills dimensions. In these organisations, 82 per cent used the Standard as an enabler to build on existing strengths and create new ones. A further 15 per cent used Investors in People as an independent good practice benchmark. The remaining three per cent used the Standard as the catalyst to achieve major turn-round. But despite the valid business reasons for embarking on the process of achieving the Standard, research shows that additional benefits ensue. It is a means to any business ends which rely on the contributions of people.

## THE TRUE COST OF TRAINING

In the organisations surveyed, net profits had grown in the preceding three years by 152 per cent in those employing fewer than 200 people, and by 90 per cent in those employing between 200 and 500 people. Higher productivity with reduced unit labour costs and increased profitability are likely outcomes from working to make reality of the statement "people are our greatest asset". Training costs money. But targeting that money to where it is needed and showing what it is buying is a natural part of the Investors in People process. Around 40 per cent of organisations using the Standard find they spend more on training and development – simply because they need to in order to meet their business objectives. Many more find that they can contain or even reduce budgets as they find smarter, more effective ways of doing things. Training doesn't necessarily mean off-the-job courses: Investors in People organisations find creative ways of training and developing their people and retaining the skills developed. The Standard gives managers and supervisors an explicit role in carrying out their training and development responsibilities. They will be supporting their people to meet their training and development needs before, during and after training.

The contribution of individuals and teams in terms of improved job performance, and how this contributes to the business itself, is tracked so that gains are measured, unnecessary spending is revealed and action to improve taken. Some of the lessons learnt from seven years' operation of Investors in People have been brought together in *Making Training Pay*, a practical toolkit developed by Investors in People UK and the Institute of Personnel and Development. The toolkit is for anyone seeking to measure and assess the contribution of training and learning to performance and is discussed in greater detail in Chapter 5.

Investors in People works in every size and type of organisation. The smallest Investor in People organisations have two or three staff – the largest has 54,000. Every sector of the economy has seen its successes with the Standard. Over 36 per cent of organisations which have achieved the Standard employ fewer than 50 people: this group normally sees benefits which are greater in extent and faster in their realisation. A similar percentage employ between 50 and 200 people. Further information on a special approach designed for smaller enterprises is contained in Chapter 6.

For every size of organisation, being an Investor in People is an important gain which earns well-deserved publicity. It sends a clear message to customers, employees, potential recruits, suppliers/supply chains and stakeholders that a rigorous and valuable National Standard has been met. Around 90 per cent of UK managers are aware of Investors in People and its impact on business relationships. Some 45 per cent of employees are aware of the Standard and what it means to their career development.

The evidence is widespread and compelling. Better people do mean better business and investing in people makes sound business sense.

## THE EFFECTS OF INVESTORS IN PEOPLE

- 62 per cent of organisations report a sharper focus for training and development.

- 59 per cent report higher motivation, pro-change attitudes and market-driven flexibility.

- 55 per cent report improved customer service, promoting brand loyalty.

- 52 per cent report clearer understanding of goals by all employees.

- 43 per cent report improved corporate image, within and outside the business.

# Chapter 5

# Making sure that training pays

**There is no point in training if it does not benefit your organisation, stresses Mike Cannell, policy advisor, the Institute of Personnel and Development**

This is not an extreme point of view. It is a sensible starting point. There have been organisations both large and small that have wasted millions of pounds, simply because although they were committed to training, they failed to put a proper plan in place and to ensure that they got results from it.

Equally, there are far too many UK organisations that have failed to invest in their people. There have been giant steps forward in recent years and the Investors in People Standard has provided a framework within which a strategic approach to training and the effectiveness of training delivery can be assessed. But, as a country, we educate and train people to a lower level than our competitors in other advanced industrialised country. And, even competitors that would be described as "newly industrialised" have plans for education and training that, if realised, are likely to take them past the UK in terms of economic achievement.

Of course, this cuts no ice with most employers and rightly so. Exhortation never did provide much, if any, incentive to employers focused on the bottom line. But it is surprising that, while the evidence of the benefits of effective training is not difficult to see, far too many organisations ignore the evidence and fail to get the benefits.

Training and development offer solid returns on investment but business attitudes to training are often sceptical. This may relate to some basic differences between human assets and physical assets. Whereas plant, machinery and buildings can be sold if they are found to be a poor purchase, training expenditure, once made, cannot be recouped. Further, it can walk or be enticed away to another employer.

On the other hand, training expenditure can be set directly against profits. It does not have to be depreciated over time. It is infinitely variable in form and delivery. From on-the-job coaching and mentoring`` via off-the-job training and education to high-tech computer and other distance-learning, training can be obtained in off-the-peg and bespoke modes, enabling means to be directly related to needs.

## BARRIERS TO TRAINING

So why do we not do more training? The answer has to be that we do not see the need to do so. Either the opportunities seem too unattractive or the threats of not doing so are too insubstantial. Arie de Geus of Royal Dutch Shell observes: "The opportunity to learn faster than your competitors may be the only sustainable competitive advantage." This may be true, but it is not a sufficiently persuasive claim unless you can see your competitors gaining an advantage at your expense.

The contribution training makes to the bottom line can easily be shown. What about the way in which the Beefeater restaurant and pub group equipped its managers to support training locally, while the Beefeater training team developed learning materials to meet various needs? As a result, improvements in customer service were noted throughout the business. The number of complaints dropped by 50 per cent and there was a substantial increase in "covers".

Or, how about the 33 per cent increase in company profits in 1992 experienced by the Victoria Wine Company, following a new management training programme that re-motivated and re-skilled managers? This resulted in stronger commitment and loyalty, and a reduction of staff turnover of 62 per cent.

Is it the case that, too often, we have simply not seen the opportunities for performance improvement that are possible?

How is it that the National Institute for Economic and Social Research was able to find that engineering plants in Holland were 30-40 per cent more productive than similar plants in Britain? In the Dutch plants 80 per cent of workers held craft qualifications. In the British plants 40 per cent were qualified. The study concluded that the Dutch workers' training made it possible to switch workers between processes much more easily.

The National Institute has carried out many other similar studies and fairly consistently found that British organisations are less efficient because the skills of their staff are of a lower order. Why should this be? Why should we not be leading the way? There are industries in which the UK leads the world and there are many world-beating companies, but not enough of them. Perhaps we simply see too few organisations that obviously base their performance on the way in which they develop their employees.

Fortunately, training is not another form of religion, in which employers believe or disbelieve. That is generally not the issue. If there is a problem it may be that employers do the minimum – training people when new investment prompts a change in skill needs – but they do not see investment as a way to release the talents of employees. And, while this may not be a matter of profound belief, it is an issue of culture.

## BENCHMARKING WITH THE BEST

The starting point, surely, for organisations which want to explore the opportunities opened up by training is an examination of their strengths and weaknesses against the best in the UK and, where the data is available, the best in the world. This may seem an impossible task, but it isn't really. The Department of Trade and Industry and many national training organisations can provide benchmarking information. Some large companies are also more than willing to provide similar information to those companies that act as suppliers to them.

Armed with this sort of output information, it is quite possible to look for the explanations of any competitiveness deficit that may be uncovered. Hopefully, however, your organisation would be found to be more effective than the benchmarks provided; if so, you are probably a convinced training organisation and likely to be an Investor in People. If you have found some other road to salvation, other than the equivalent of a pot of gold in the ground, you will no doubt keep it to yourself.

There are many routes that can be taken to identify training needs, but basically these are either: strategic – looking broadly at the future needs and positioning of the organisation; or tactical – taking issues as they arise. Inevitably, even the best organisations do both but the strategic route is very important. It is difficult to see how any organisation can become a market leader unless its approach is strategic.

## MEASURING THE BENEFITS

Training and development leads to substantial, measurable, performance benefits. Measuring the benefits of some types of training intervention is relatively easy. Improvements in output per head, in reduced re-work, staff/customer ratios, time to market, etc. can be directly quantified, and forecast savings or enhanced revenue flows can be set against the costs of the training and tracked to the bottom line.

Other benefits of training have to be measured indirectly. Think about improvements in customer satisfaction and quality. They have both direct and indirect benefits. There are tangible benefits such as reductions in returns. But there are intangible, and arguably more important, benefits such as the enhanced reputation which organisations enjoy that go beyond the "here and now" to give long-lasting competitive advantage.

Being strategic can mean going beyond the sorts of specific training that, for instance, help people to use time more effectively, reach a higher level of competence in a simple repetitive task, or become skilled in a related task to improve flexibility. In many cases it has to do with development rather than training, ie. something which may enhance employees' vision, widen their understanding of the business or prepare them to make an upward career move within the organisation. Such an intervention may affect whole departments and whole workforces. The open-learning facilities introduced by organisations such as Rover and Unipart fall into this category.

Again, being strategic may have to do with the development or strengthening of the core competences of the organisation. Research conducted for the IPD highlighted that companies with sophisticated training systems look to training to support corporate strategy and change more often than they look for measurable financial returns on investment. The term "pay forward" (in comparison with the nearly immediate pay-back of more specific training) was invented to help make this distinction.

A firm of insurance brokers defined the secret of success as: "Not cutting corners and lowering standards but improving service and value to customers". Staff development was identified as a fundamental part of the process. Among the benefits they identified from investing in learning were: reduced staff turnover; a 20-per-cent improvement in policy renewal retentions; and a 15-per-cent increase in profitability and improved teamworking. They have achieved Investors in People recognition.

Another example of an organisation that has invested heavily is a house-building firm that cited one of the benefits of apprentice training investment as being the development of a public image as a socially responsible firm and an integral part of the local community. This built their "quality" reputation in their local market. The challenge of training is not doing it but getting competitive benefit from it. The starting point should be the search for competitive advantage and an analysis of everybody's needs. The pace is hotting up; don't be the last to find out that better strategic planning of training pays.

*The Institute of Personnel and Development and Investors in People UK have developed Making Training Pay, a toolkit to assist with the planning and evaluation of training. For more details, see page 80.*

# Chapter 6

# Building a better business

**Joan MacFarlane, a director of Esteem, a company which has worked closely with Investors in People UK and Scottish Enterprise in developing and implementing a toolkit aimed specifically at smaller businesses**

To stay ahead in an ever-changing market, firms need to ensure that they have the right people in the right jobs doing the right things with the right information, the right skills and the right leadership. In doing so they will keep all their people motivated to do their best and be flexible enough to meet the increasing demands made by customers.

Investors in People has proved to be a successful approach for organisations of all sizes and from all sectors of the economy. An increasing number of small businesses are finding the Standard particularly useful in planning for the future and implementing activities which drive the business forward.

To support small firms further in their use of Investors in People, Investors in People UK and Scottish Enterprise developed the *Building a Better Business* toolkit which was launched in July 1997. The programme was created to help small businesses face the challenges which they encounter every day as they grow, develop or in some cases, face a battle for survival. It also enables companies to achieve the Standard in an easy-to-understand, business focused, step-by-step way which can be tailored to meet differing business priorities. Written in plain English, the toolkit provides practical support in a simple, user-friendly, framework for companies to build a solid foundation and develop a blueprint for their business. This, in turn, allows each company to grow, develop and be successful.

The key features of the *Building a Better Business* toolkit are:

■ Introduction
*This provides an overview of each element, indicating where to start and who to contact for assistance;*

■ Where is your business now?
*A questionnaire, giving employers an indication of what they already have in place and which areas need to be worked on;*

■ Eight elements
*A concise narrative around each of the eight elements of the pack (detailed below) with practical examples;*

■ Starter-for-10
*A floppy disk containing practical examples which can be modified to suit the needs of the business.*

This is how *Building a Better Business* can help with some of the growing pains experienced by businesses:

| Issue | Common experience | Toolkit section |
|-------|-------------------|-----------------|
| Focus | When we start our business we are very focused on what it is we want to do, how we want to do it, why we are doing it, where we want it to take us, who our customers are, our products etc. Do you ever feel you and your staff sometimes lose sight of this? | **Business direction** <br> A step-by-step approach to help you to focus on your strategic direction and leadership and then communicate the direction to your staff |
| Measuring success and failure | Do you measure your successes and failures? Do you know what you and your business are achieving? Are your staff clear about what it is that you are doing in order to achieve your business direction? | **Key results** <br> Helps you to set your business objectives/goals/ aims/targets and to communicate them to staff. The key results will allow you tomeasure your progress, and be the first port of call to identify skills, knowledge, attitude and behaviour gaps in your business |

| Issue | Common experience | Toolkit section |
|-------|-------------------|-----------------|
| Employing people | Are you meeting your legal requirements of employing staff? Do you have personnel policies in place to protect your business and its employees? | **Your people**<br>Looks at what to consider having in place and how to go about it |
| New people | Do you give your new members of staff the right information at the right time to make them effective quickly enough? Have you set them up for success? Or do you wonder why it takes so long for new members of staff to be effective? What is your business like for new people who join?<br>When was the last time you undertook a new venture or new skill? Do you remember how you felt? How do you handle staff changing roles? | **Employees in new jobs**<br>Helps you to set each employee up for success by pre-planning what they need, when they need it, who should provide it and how it should happen. This should allow each employee who is new or changing role to become effective more quickly and therefore have an impact on your business |
| Effective training | Have you ever paid for staff training only to find later that it has been a waste of time, money and effort? | **Training & development**<br>This looks at the Training Cycle, asking the following questions:<br>How can you identify training and development needs? (see Key Results)<br>How can you select the right method of fulfilling them?<br>How can you ensure staff are clear about the purpose of the training and what is expected after it?<br>How can you measure the impact it has had on performance, skills and your business as a whole? |

| Issue | Common experience | Toolkit section |
|---|---|---|
| Managing people | Most people do not set up in business because they like to manage people. It comes with the territory! | **Managing performance** Helps you to look at how you manage staff and maintain morale and motivation? How do staff know what they are achieving and how this is contributing to the success of the business? How do you review their progress? How do you know what their training and development needs are? How do you focus them on the future? |
| Planning for success | As the saying goes, "If you fail to plan you plan to fail!" And this goes a long way beyond the existence or absence of a business plan. Have you looked at the big picture of what you are trying to achieve in each area? How does this all fit together? Are you being too ambitious or not ambitious enough? | **Plan for the business** This will give practical advice on what should be in an effective Plan for the Business to enable it to become a living tool which provides you with focus and is a benchmark to check your progress against. |

The final element not described above is the External Review. This is the external benchmark of the Investors in People Standard. It is by continually improving their performance in each of these areas that small firms can stay competitive and efficient.

As you will see from all of the above, building a better business is not rocket science, just simple common sense. The case study overleaf highlights a company that has used the *Building a Better Business* toolkit to achieve recognition as Investors in People.

## CASE STUDY

### Recognised as an Investor in People May 1997

No. of employees:       18
No. of sites:           2
Date company started:   April 1995
Type of business:       Limited company

Carousel Nurseries opened in April 1995 at the Leven Valley Enterprise Centre. A second nursery in Alexandria opened in March 1996. It is currently run by two partners, Anne Jenkins and Claire Rowan.

The nurseries are decorated in the "Carousel" theme – with curtains, borders and wall displays portraying a bright and stimulating environment for children to enjoy – and provide facilities for children aged between six weeks and eight years.

Carousel Nurseries used the Building a Better Business toolkit to achieve the Investors in People Standard. Throughout the implementation period, the business to continued to function as usual and the women were able to build sufficient momentum to achieve "ownership" of every stage at an early point in the process.

### Business benefits
The company benefited in the following ways:

- Key results achieved;

- Staff more focused;

- Staff feeling more involved and better able to make a contribution;

- Company profile raised;

- Claire and Anne feel as if they have been "professionally developed";

- Company partners now leading by example;

- Increased awareness from all staff about what they should be aspiring to;

### Continuous improvement
"Everyone knows that the goal-posts are ever moving. We now have the foundation to grow and develop with the systems and good practice we have in place, and these change on a continual basis, as does our business." Claire Rowan, partner, Carousel Nurseries.

# Chapter 7

# The director's role

How should directors be taking a lead on people issues?
Geraint Day, IoD business research officer and Mark Watson,
IoD corporate governance executive, offer some tips

How often have you said that your company's most valuable
assets are your employees? Probably quite often. Indeed, when
one stops to think about it, as every day passes, your employees
become more valuable to the company, as they learn new skills
and develop new ideas about how to do their job more
effectively. Your employees, therefore, have an amazing potential
to provide your company with a real competitive advantage.

Yet, how often have you stopped to consider whether you
are providing your employees with effective leadership. And,
how regularly have you taken the time and allocated the
necessary resources to find out what your employees know and
feel? This chapter provides you with some food for thought on
effective leadership, and offers advice on how to assess your
employees' attitudes and put the findings to best use.

## TAKING THE LEAD

As a director, you will know that in deciding how best to take
the company forward, the board must be clear about where it
wants the company to be in the future, determine clear objectives
to get there and in doing so set the framework within which
clear, discrete plans can be identified and implemented. In addition
to being clear and unambiguous, these plans must be measurable
so that performance in achieving them can be evaluated.

You should also recognise that in taking forward any plans
within your company, the board of directors must provide
leadership. As a board member, you must be seen to champion
key elements of the corporate plan, providing the necessary
resources to ensure that maximum results are achieved. As

INSTITUTE OF DIRECTORS

# *Guidelines*
# FOR DIRECTORS

## Best selling book published by the IoD for over 20 years.

*DO YOU KNOW*

- How a director's duties are defined by the law?
- How a board operates?
- What the law expects of director?
- What information a company must disclose?
- How a director can lose office?
- Who the law can treat as a director?

## A practical guide to the role, duties and responsibilities of a director

To order your copy, simply send a cheque for £16.50 (includes p&p) or your credit card details to:

Publications Department
The Director Publications Limited
116 Pall Mall, London SW1Y 5ED
Telephone: 0171 766 8766
(Goods will only be dispatched on receipt of payment)

organisational psychologist, Professor Cary Cooper of the Manchester School of Management, put it when posing a question for directors and managers, "Can organisations demand commitment from employees when they themselves fail to commit to their employees?"

Leadership can mean many things, but if one were to list those characteristics considered important, these might include motivator, communicator or delegator. While the list could go on, one would soon find that each implies a relationship with other people – primarily your employees. This inter-personal element also suggests that there is no one way to provide effective leadership. Instead, it is a dynamic, two-way process, wherein you influence individual and organisational performance through your relationships with those around you.

## GETTING TO KNOW YOUR EMPLOYEES

In addition to promoting regular two-way communications with your employees, your board could consider surveying your employees' attitudes. Such surveys could be based on broad general issues, or focused on specific matters, such as a proposed change in working practices. Whatever the focus, you must be clear about the objectives of the survey, and ensure that, from the beginning, employees are informed of these objectives. Successfully embarking on the Investor in People Standard, for example, requires the full support of your employees, which will only be achieved by involving them from the outset.

In deciding to survey your employees' attitudes, you must communicate the processes involved, and perhaps more importantly, explain where the survey and its result fit into the company's long-term strategy. It is the resulting action which is important, not the survey itself.

Above all, don't try to seek the views of your employees unless you intend to take the findings seriously and consider making changes as a result. You wouldn't consider wasting resources elsewhere in your company, so why should you when it comes to assessing your employees' views. Undertaking an employee attitude survey with no rationale wastes resources and can demotivate staff who feel that their views have simply been noted, but then ignored. Deciding to research and benefit from surveys of employees' attitudes is, in this sense, no different from defining financial objectives.

### SURVEYING EMPLOYEE ATTITUDES

As a director you may or may not be involved in the detail of the survey. However, it is important that you know that your company doesn't have to start from scratch in designing and undertaking employee attitude surveys. Several of the organisations mentioned in this Guide, such as the Institute of Personnel and Development, and the Department of Trade and Industry, have expertise in conducting such surveys.

While the size of the survey affects the mechanics and processes, the general principles of surveys are the same. You must first agree clear objectives and then define ways of measuring outcomes. There are too many instances of organisations doing surveys, getting back hundreds of questionnaires, only to discover that nobody had given proper thought to how the returns were to be analysed, how the results are to be presented and when they are needed by. Even the art of writing questions needs to be considered – as the saying goes, ask a silly question and get a silly answer. If you don't have the skills in-house to undertake a survey, try the local further education college or university, the local TEC (Training and Enterprise Council) or one of the national bodies mentioned in this Director's Guide.

Remember, undertaking an employee attitude survey involves resources (including time) and you should try to get the best use of these. So if you were thinking about issuing a self-completion questionnaire, you need to ensure that the right people are involved in drawing up the questions, physically producing and sending out the forms, and gathering in the results. Above all, don't forget the need to ensure board-level commitment to the process. The table overleaf summarises some of the essentials.

## EMPLOYEE ATTITUDES SURVEY: SOME FACTORS TO CONSIDER

| Area | Comments |
| --- | --- |
| What are the objectives? | Decide what you are trying to achieve |
| What issues do you want to include? | Attitudes to: the organisation, to its management, customers, competitors or other areas? |
| Who will be surveyed? | Everybody, or a statistical sample of employees |
| Get board commitment | Crucial: don't go ahead otherwise |
| Let employees know what is going on | May need to dispel suspicions |
| Decide survey method | Self-completion questionnaire? Will it be anonymous? – will probably get more frank (and more useful) responses |
| Draw up and agree questions | May need to test questions out as a pilot: talk to a statistician even at this stage |
| Send out questionnaire | Ensure confidentiality |
| Collect the returns | Ensure confidentiality |
| Data entry from returns | Use suitable computer software |
| Analyse returns | Use suitable computer software |
| More detailed analysis | As necessary: use statistical advice |
| Present report | Written or oral, to the board? |
| Discuss any actions | Board and management, perhaps ongoing with employees |
| Feedback to employees | Very important or cynicism may result |

See: Incomes Data Services ("IDS Studies Plus: Employee attitude surveys", January 1998); also Department of Trade and Industry, and Department for Education and Employment ("Competitiveness through partnerships with people", 1997).

## ACTING ON THE RESULTS

Once you get the results of the survey, you must act on them. If necessary, refer back to earlier documentation to refresh yourself and your fellow directors why the survey was undertaken in the first place. Above all, remember that the actions undertaken following the survey are far more important than undertaking the survey itself. Decide what needs to be done to ensure that the survey is used most effectively to achieve the desired objectives. It may be that, in the short term, little substantive change is possible. The findings may even suggest that further research is necessary. Whatever the outcome, employees must be kept informed all along of the survey's results and the actions that will be forthcoming from the findings.

Surveying your employees is only a small part of providing them with effective leadership. Investing in your employees through training, being seen to reward them fairly for their commitment, considering new and innovative ways to make their work lives more fulfilling – these are some of the other roles of the board vis-à-vis their employees, many of which are discussed in detail in this Directors' Guide.

Yet, if your employees really are your company's most valuable assets, finding out what they think and feel is a vital part of realising their worth. This chapter should have given you a flavour of the factors that you should consider in surveying their attitudes. It should also have shown that the survey itself is will only prove effective if it has a clear rationale and its findings are put to best use.

In starting the whole process of surveying employees, you show your employees that not only do you value their skills, but also that you are concerned about them as people. Handled well, such surveys should provide plentiful data on which to base key operational and strategic decisions. They should also improve the attitudes of the employees as results lead to changes, albeit, in some cases, in the long term.

Above all, the survey should be used positively to build greater trust between the company's board and senior management and its employees. Only by involving your employees, and being seen to do so, will you truly realise the potential competitive advantage that your employees can give your company.

# Chapter 8

# The quality factor

**Malcolm Franks, chief executive, the British Quality Foundation, explains how harnessing the skills and talents of everyone in a company can play a pivotal role in success or failure**

Today, business excellence in all its aspects has never been more relevant. All organisations have to respond positively to global market pressures just to stand still, let alone improve their performance.

Increasingly, excellence is being seen as a "hard" issue, something which can improve both the bottom line and the quality of life for all involved in organisations which take continuous improvement seriously. It's a common mistake to regard excellence, or quality-related issues, as mainly to do with processes. Nothing could be further from the truth. Harnessing "people power" to improve product, service and management standards lies at the heart of any successful company. In simple terms, a company can have the best processes in the world, but it won't succeed unless it maximises the potential of its people.

## HELP IS AT HAND

Any company which wants to improve the management and motivation of its people can get help and advice from a range of sources – ISO 9000, Investors in People, Charter Mark, Tomorrow's Company, Management Charter Initiative and the Department of Trade and Industry's Best Practice Services – to name but a few. These initiatives often stand alone within an organisation, and management and staff may not know how they link together.

However, one framework – the Business Excellence Model – can link all of these standards and help companies put individual quality initiatives into the context of an overall business improvement strategy. One of the strongest links between these

AMP GB   Anglian Water   Associated British Ports   Avis Rent A Car   Barclays Bank
Bechtel   Beneficial Bank   BG Transco   Birmingham Midshires   Bovis Europe
BP Chemicals   Bristol Quality Centre   British Car Auctions   British Gas   British
Telecommunications Caradon Commercial Union Assurance Courtaulds Department
of Trade & Industry  DHL International (UK)  Exel Logistics  Friends' Provident Life Office
Gardner Merchant  Glaxo Wellcome  Group 4  Guardian Insurance  Halifax  Hewlett-
Packard  IBM United Kingdom  ICL  IMI  ICI  Independent Insurance Co  International
Petroleum  Exchange   Jaguar  Cars   John  Laing   Lafarge  Redland  Aggregates

# If you're serious

about business, you need to think about

# the company you keep

Leicestershire Mental Health Service NHS  Lever Brothers  Lloyds TSB Group  Magnox
Electric  Marks and Spencer  Midland Bank  National Westminster Bank  Nicholas Clarke
Investments Limited  Nissan Motor Manufacturing (UK) Ltd  Nortel  Nuclear Electric
Pentland Group   Pirelli Cables   RAC Motoring Services   Rover Group   Royal &
SunAlliance UK Life  Securicor  SGS United Kingdom  SmithKline Beecham  Smurfit
Standard Chartered Group Tarmac Texas Instruments The British Standards Institution
The  National  Grid  Company   The  Post  Office   TNT  UK   Unilever  UK   Unipart
United Utilities  Vauxhall Motors  Warburg Dillon Read  Xerox (UK)  Zeneca Group

All these organisations have one thing in common - each one is a Founder Member of the British
Quality Foundation. To find out more about how the Foundation can help your business, contact
Malcolm Franks, Chief Executive, British Quality Foundation, 32-34 Great Peter Street,
London SW1P 2QX   Tel: 0171 654 5000

Website www.quality-foundation.co.uk
e-mail malcolm.franks@quality-foundation.co.uk

British Quality
Foundation

initiatives and the Business Excellence Model is the emphasis they all place on harnessing the potential of people.

There is no right or best way, to address better people management. Companies should choose the method which best fits their culture. However, self-assessment against the Business Excellence Model is one of the most accessible and powerful management tools currently available to highlight all the aspects which contribute to an organisation's success, including, of course, people management.

The Model (see overleaf) is based on some very simple assumptions, namely that Customer Satisfaction, People (employee) Satisfaction and Impact on Society are achieved through Leadership driving Policy and Strategy, People Management, Resources and Processes leading, ultimately, to excellence in business results. The use of the Model is promoted in the UK by the British Quality Foundation.

### A GUIDE, NOT A SOLUTION

The Model isn't prescriptive. It doesn't tell organisations what to do, but instead provides guidelines which enable an organisation to pursue excellence on its own terms, taking into account its own circumstances, at its own pace. It consists of nine elements. These elements are grouped into two broad areas:

■ *Enablers – HOW we do things;*

■ *Results – WHAT we target, measure and achieve.*

Each of these nine elements represents an area of activity within an organisation which contributes to its success. By regularly reviewing both the activities and the results in these areas, an organisation can test its progress towards business excellence.

One of the key Enablers is People Management, which addresses how the organisation releases the full potential of its people. In this instance, the term "people" is defined as all the individuals employed by the organisation, and any others who participate in the task of serving its customers, directly or indirectly.

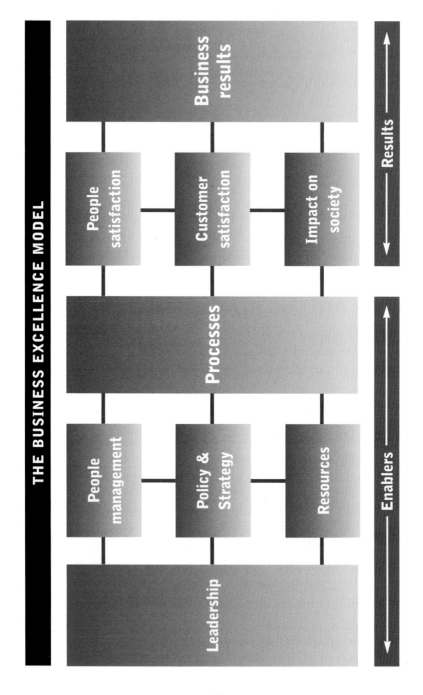

# THE BUSINESS EXCELLENCE MODEL

Leadership

People management

Policy & Strategy

Resources

Processes

People satisfaction

Customer satisfaction

Impact on society

Business results

Enablers

Results

Under People Management, the Model asks a company to look at:

- *How people resources are planned and improved;*
- *How their capabilities are sustained and developed;*
- *How people agree targets and review performance;*
- *How people are involved, empowered and recognised;*
- *How people and the organisation have an effective dialogue;*
- *How people are cared for.*

People Management asks an organisation to consider whether:

- *Individuals are sufficiently trained, and their abilities recognised;*
- *People have a good understanding of how their particular job benefits the business;*
- *Everyone knows clearly which tasks have priority;*
- *There are ways of recognising people who become involved in improvement;*
- *There are regular meetings which all staff have the opportunity to attend.*

Activity is all very well, but what matters are results and the Model groups the results of People Management activities under the heading of People Satisfaction – in other words, what the organisation is achieving in relation to the satisfaction of its people. Under People Satisfaction, the Model asks a company to look at its employees' perception of the organisation. People Satisfaction asks a company to consider whether:

- *People enjoy working for the company and display a high degree of loyalty;*
- *Absence levels and staff turnover show improving trends;*
- *People are very willing to become involved in trying to improve the business.*

At first glance these questions may seem obvious, but it's surprising how many organisations don't address people satisfaction issues in any formal or effective way. While self-assessment against the Model can provide the framework, it's up to organisations to take the initiative.

## ASSESSING YOUR BUSINESS

One of the best ways to undertake self-assessment against the Model is to use ASSESS, a suite of software and paper-based products from the British Quality Foundation. It is the only self-assessment product to be mapped directly onto the Model and is one of the best ways to unlock its power.

ASSESS can help companies address many of the key people-related issues which make the difference between success and failure in the marketplace. It can be used to review an entire organisation, or a department, division or operational unit and doesn't require any specialised knowledge to use successfully. ASSESS delivers a range of quantifiable benefits, including more focused leadership, the development of concise action plans and the greater motivation of people.

In addition to this self-assessment product, the British Quality Foundation offers a range of other products and services to help companies address people management and motivational issues. The Foundation works closely with the DTI on many initiatives and the DTI also offers a range of complementary products and services aimed at helping companies with people-related issues.

Along with the BQF, the DTI also sees the promotion of business excellence as a key objective. This reflects the close association that has existed between the BQF and the DTI since the former was established in 1992. The DTI was instrumental in this process through the provision of funding in the BQF's earlier years. To reinforce this commitment, the DTI became a founder member of the BQF earlier this year, and is represented on its board and executive.

Business Excellence is seen by the DTI as an ideal framework for continuous improvement for all types of organisation and it, therefore, promotes business excellence through a range of facilitated services that are designed to spread best practice to small and medium- sized enterprises (SMEs).

## THREE KEY BEST PRACTICE INITIATIVES FROM THE DTI

### CONNECT FOR BETTER BUSINESS

The DTI's award-winning Connect for Better Business (CBB) – a CD Rom-based service of ten interactive CD modules which promote an awareness of best practice issues. The range includes a new Partnership with People module which covers issues such as shared goals, shared culture, shared learning, shared effort and shared information (See chapter 1 for more on Partnerships with People). Increasingly, companies are recognising that their most important resource is their people.

There is a new partnership ethos emerging within companies which is creating a different type of organisation from the "command and control" structures with which we have been familiar in the past. The most successful companies are seeking to explore ways to create an environment in which people can thrive and seek success for themselves and their organisations. The CDs, which can be used in presentations, one-to-one sessions, seminars and the like, can provide companies with an impetus to improve their performance by learning from the experience of others.

### UNITED KINGDOM BENCHMARKING INDEX

SMEs can measure their performance against that of their competitors through the United Kingdom Benchmarking Index (UKBI). This is a comprehensive, facilitated, computer-based service which allows comparisons to be made in around 80 aspects of performance – not only on hard management and financial data, but also against the nine elements of the Business Excellence Model. Both the business excellence and management sections of the UKBI's questionnaire enable a company's performance to be assessed in the key areas of People Management and People Satisfaction, such as staff turnover, training, accident rates, etc. Currently, about 1,000 SMEs have been benchmarked using the Index, resulting in the largest database of SME benchmarking information in Europe.

## INSIDE UK ENTERPRISE

The third in the DTI's range of best practice services to SMEs is Inside UK Enterprise (IUKE). This offers the opportunity to experience, at first hand, the implementation of best practice through a programme of visits to exemplar companies. IUKE is a major component in the DTI's support for business. It is endorsed by the CBI and is the largest scheme of its type in the world. Most host companies who take part in the programme are experienced in implementing and operating one or more aspects of best practice, and many use the Business Excellence Model. The host companies are drawn from a broad cross-section of UK manufacturing and service sectors. Visitors can choose companies in relevant market sectors, or areas of management expertise, including human resources, where they can see a broad range of best practice in action.

Taken together, the help available from the BQF and the DTI to any company which seriously wants to harness the power of its people is considerable. More information about the products and services that are available from the British Quality Foundation and the DTI can be found in the appendices.

# Chapter 9

# People down the line

**There Are many interrelating factors which influence the development of a world-class supply chain, but one common factor has a major impact – people. Peter Russian, product development manager of Investors in People UK, reports**

With ever-increasing competition in the market place, the importance of having access to world-class suppliers has never been more critical. An outstanding supply chain is fast becoming the decisive factor for business success and there are many organisations that exemplify this – Nissan and Toyota in the automotive industry and Marks & Spencer in the retail sector are commonly-quoted examples.

People management and Investors in People are usually seen as internal disciplines that help an organisation gain a competitive advantage over its rivals. However, recent research shows that 73 per cent of organisations believe that they would benefit if other companies – namely their suppliers – were committed to the Investors in People Standard. Why are these organisations interested in their suppliers working with the Investors in People? And how can you think big when it comes to your supply chain?

## WORKING ON THE CHAIN GANG

No man is an island and no organisation can stand on its own. We all need to work with other organisations, either as buyers or suppliers. From the car manufacturer to the supermarket, and the garage owner to the local shop, we all work with organisations.

Most companies which purchase goods from suppliers on a regular basis will identify critical measures that the supplier needs to meet. These may include delivery time, cost, and flexibility to respond to new requirements. Any change in the quality of the service provided may have serious implications for both suppliers – whose business will rely on establishing and maintaining long-term arrangements with clients – and buyers who are reliant on the quality of supplier to deliver a product or service to their customer.

Most organisations see people development and management as internal issues. If we accept that people can play a critical part in the drive for improved quality in an organisation, should we not place more importance on how people, and therefore services, are managed in our suppliers? Equally, if a company can demonstrate that the way in which their organisation is managed is in line with a national benchmark of good practice, they will present a more attractive alternative to prospective buyers.

## SUPPLY CHAIN MANAGEMENT

The importance of supply chain management is growing. In the UK's most successful companies, the relationships between buyer and supplier are based on partnership, not conflict. These organisations are taking growing responsibility for the development of suppliers. They believe that suppliers form part of a "virtual organisation", and that developing the skills and acumen of their suppliers contributes towards a continuous cycle of improvement, and ultimately fuels growth and profitability. So, large organisations can play a significant role in supporting the development of their supply chain. However, in choosing suppliers, a purchaser may look for evidence of commitment to business improvement in a company, ie. the potential for development in an organisation. A commitment to work towards the Investors in People Standard will be an indication of an organisation's commitment towards improvement, and the likely effectiveness of a joint development programme.

Of course smaller organisations will not have the capacity to be so proactive in developing their supply chains as large multinationals like EEV, Unipart, Michelin and BT. But smaller companies are even more vulnerable to changes and inconsistency in the quality of the service or product provided by their suppliers. You need to be certain that a new supplier won't let you down through poor production or bad management.

External quality awards won't guarantee that your supplier won't let you down, but they will indicate that an organisation has taken appropriate action to improve and maintain certain systems and procedures. ISO 9000 is the most commonly used quality award in the selection of suppliers. The award demonstrates that a company has taken the appropriate steps to ensure that the processes that underpin its activities are appropriate.

The Investors in People Standard is unique. It is the only quality standard that addresses the way in which people work in an organisation. It provides external recognition to companies which understand the critical path their employees can play in delivering their business objectives. Most importantly, Investors in People is about attitude and commitment. An organisation won't be recognised if it can't show true commitment to the principles of the Standard; in other words, it cannot be imposed on a company, and it cannot be treated with lip service. As a buyer what can you expect from an Investor in People? The performance related benefits experienced by Investors in People are:

■ *A better quality of customer service;*

■ *Reduced costs;*

■ *Improved delivery to specification;*

■ *Increased reliability of delivery.*

All of these benefits can clearly be passed onto buyers, which will ultimately result in their own increased profitability.

### WORKING FOR YOUR CUSTOMERS

So, how can you maintain and grow your business effectively using the Investors in People Standard? Start off by looking at what it is that you can do better than any of your competitors, and that will make your company stand out for potential customers. Ask yourself the following:

- *How much do you know about your competitors?*

- *What quality models and standards do they use to ensure the effectiveness of their organisation?*

- *If they don't appear to use any standards how can you steal a march on them?*

By committing your organisation to becoming an Investor in People you will show your customers that you're serious about getting the quality of your goods or services right.

Some of your customers, especially if they are larger firms, may well be Investors in People themselves. Ask them for help and advice about working towards the Standard. They will know only too well that it is to their benefit also, if you are committed to becoming an Investor in People.

## WORKING WITH YOUR SUPPLIERS

By seeing the benefits of developing your people you'll understand better how this can affect your customers and suppliers. To paraphrase a famous soap powder advertising campaign: "Are you really happy with the quality of your suppliers?"

There is almost certainly some room for improvement in the goods or services that they provide, and it is likely that the people in the company can make a difference. Find out more about your supplier's commitment towards organisational and business development – look for commitment to becoming, or recognition as, an Investor in People as a sign of the quality of the organisation.

Join or help to form a network of suppliers, and use these as an opportunity to exchange ideas and learn new ways in which to improve your organisation.

## CASE STUDY

EEV Ltd is a wholly owned subsidiary of GEC and is the UK's largest professional electron tube company. It exports half of its annual sales of around £80m to 70 companies worldwide. As a key player in a competitive technological market, EEV has to maintain the highest quality standards in all of its products.

### Supplier strategy

To support the manufacturing process the company buys some £9m worth of metal components each year from a range of specialist engineering companies. Preferred suppliers must fulfil strict criteria. When rigorous quality control systems revealed that some valued suppliers were failing to comply with EEV requirements, the company decided to contribute towards the development of suppliers which would be to their mutual benefit.

Work within EEV to achieve the Investors in People Standard began in 1993. The company believes in sharing its vision with its suppliers: both staff and suppliers are kept up to date with corporate and technical information, and supplier briefing meetings bring together competing suppliers. In this way, expectations are made explicit, horizons are raised and competitiveness is fostered. Making the links with Investors in People experiences prompted EEV to look at its suppliers' whole business arrangements against the Standard, not simply the skills.

Now supplier development activity is an addition to the company's comprehensive range of training in management and engineering skills. At present, EEV is directly supporting two suppliers working towards Investors in People – Lema Engineering and BDR Instruments.

### The benefits

With a new approach to supplier development at EEV, new types of relationships with suppliers have developed:

- Longer-term alliances have been built, giving reassurance on both sides (eg. in investment);

- Suppliers' competitiveness, flexibility and business skills and systems have been enhanced; higher quality work is delivered with reduced non-conformance; greater flexibility of supply to meet market fluctuations has been achieved;

- Sourcing and component costs have been reduced.

# Best Practice Services

If you have an interest in business improvement, best practice or business excellence and would like to find out more about how the DTI can help you, please telephone, e-mail, or fax any of the contacts listed below.

General enquiries

## Connect for Better Business
David Turner
tel: 0171 215 3917  fax: 0171 215 2877
e-mail: dave.turner@rsme.dti.gov.uk

## United Kingdom Benchmarking Index
Paul Groninger
tel: 0171 215 3915  fax: 0171 215 2877
e-mail: paul.groninger@rsme.dti.gov.uk

## Inside UK Enterprise
John Launchbury
tel: 0171 215 3916  fax: 0171 215 2877
e-mail: john.launchbury@rsme.dti.gov.uk

Department of Trade and Industry

# Chapter 10

# Putting it into practice

**John Lawless, a regular contributor to The Sunday Times, singles out three companies which have taken people partnerships seriously**

Barry Dodd quit his job as an ICI graduate trainee in 1973 because, "In a big company, I could never seriously affect the outcome of things". When he launched his own industrial labelling company, GSM a year later, he vowed that all employees would have an opportunity to make an impact. His initiative could not have been more unfashionable. Industrialists were running scared of trades unions and avoiding any close contact with their workforce and soon after Britain would suffer its worst-ever period of industrial unrest, during "the winter of discontent".

Although Dodd's experiment was to exceed his greatest expectations, the defining moment was to come two decades later. Two GSM workers, being interviewed for an Investors in People Award, declared: "Barry doesn't run GSM. We all do."

For Dodd, sole shareholder in GSM, apparently losing control of his fast-growth, very nicely profitable and debt-free, £10m sales-a-year company was a triumph. For he is convinced that GSM has survived and prospered – unlike four rivals it has bought out of receivership in the nineties – simply because it has developed the ultimate partnership with its employees.

GSM employs more than 200 people at factories in Thirsk, Wetherby and Brecon. "They are totally responsible for their own operations," says Dodd, "and for preserving the uniqueness of GSM's culture. Without that, we risk losing everything."

As it grows bigger, GSM has to work harder to keep a smallness of character and culture which maintains a flexibility, nimbleness and keeps it close to its customers. Unlike so many companies, which seek economies of scale by concentrating their production into large units, GSM deliberately keeps manufacturing divided between its three geographically-distinct sites. The Brecon site is dedicated to supplying the car makers, with Wetherby serving electronics companies and Thirsk supplying up to 2,000 small-order customers.

"We said we would never have more than 100 people at any one site," says Andrew Hall, who joined Dodd as his general manager in 1987, having previously worked at tailoring firm, Hepworth. "It had up to 2,500 people making clothes in one room. You couldn't even begin to communicate with people. Far from achieving economies of scale, it brought high overheads. Barry and I determined that people are only motivated by being involved." Adds Dodd: "We effectively have three companies, but group strength."

### FLATTENING THE HIERARCHY

Each factory has six highly-focused teams. Team leaders gather at 7.50am every working day and are briefed about the state of GSM's whole business: order levels, delivery targets (and how they are being met), investment programmes, profitability and much more. Even potential acquisitions are discussed. "When I thought about diversifying into an unrelated field," says Dodd, relishing the memory, "a lot of down-to-earth Yorkshiremen and Welshmen shot that idea down in flames." The leaders then brief their teams. "We have one of the flattest management structures possible," adds Dodd.

Staying small business-minded and alert means that GSM can track changes in customer demand. So much so, that its product range – which in the early nineties was confined to millions of labels to go on car chassis, computer frames and cookers – has now developed to encompass oven doors (to which manufacturers simply add their controls) and a system that allows one major automobile manufacturer to define the differing production requirements for each car made via pre-printed plastic labels attached to the bodyshell. Dodd and Hall encourage workers to visit customers and other GSM factories. But empowering staff in companies that have been taken over doesn't happen overnight. Four years ago when the Brecon factory was acquired, workers there still insisted on having clocking-on clocks – even though they have been abandoned everywhere else within GSM. "Talking to outsiders becomes ever easier," says Hall. "You can put stuff onto a CD-Rom and zap it out. But maintaining our style and the way we operate, by talking to people inside, is hard work. You have to make it happen all the time."

## THE AMERICAN WAY

For Barrie Payne, at Sunrise Medical, the belief in partnership with people is as strong. But the way in which its 4,000 staff worldwide are motivated could not be more distinctively different. Sunrise Medical sells more than £400m worth of rehabilitation and homecare equipment a year – ranging from lifts and breathing aids to Zimmer frames, trendy-looking scooters and thousands of wheelchairs. The company has 880 employees at its 370,000 sq ft factory at Wollaston in the West Midlands, which was opened in March 1998 by the Princess Royal. But motivation techniques used there (and at all Sunrise sites worldwide) very much reflect the company's American parentage.

All workers are known as "associates" and no job titles are allowed to have capital letters. Staff are urged to have B-HAGs. "Everybody is encouraged to have big, hairy or audacious goals," says Payne, "like doubling production." But when somebody actually does something above and beyond the call of corporate duty – like a 17-year-old secretary who worked through her lunch hour to produce urgently-needed minutes – they get sent a mock telegram, known within Sunrise as an "Exceedogram". Bright ideas are rewarded with lumens (which take their name from the measure of light). A bronze lumen is worth one raffle ticket, a silver two and a gold three. Prizes include holidays and a car.

Payne believes in "management by walking", getting out and about from his office for at least 30 minutes every day. And the tide of involvement also flows the other way. As electronics board assembler Christine Connelly stresses: "If I feel like it, I know I can call Barrie and arrange a meeting to discuss absolutely anything." In the month of their birthday, all associates are invited to a sandwiches-and-Coke lunch with Payne. "They ask any questions they like and I guarantee them honest answers," he says.

Gorilla awards are handed out at annual conferences for sales, production, R&D and customer service teams who have flown in from around the globe to challenge each other to say what they have done that is remarkable. "These are our industrial Oscars," says Payne. "We used to give cheques out with them. Now we don't need to. People really care about the recognition they give them. British managers feel awkward about such things, of course, but the funny thing is, when I was given one, I couldn't help it, I really loved it."

Do fun-things actually work? Sunrise Medical has had 20 per cent growth in each year for 11 years and has achieved a 44 per cent return on capital invested. Its associates get "a piece of pie", a participation in earnings worth 4 per cent to 8 per cent of annual bonuses.

## PARTNERSHIPS IN THE EXTREME

By contrast, when Jim Anderson, general manager of operations at ITW DeVilbiss, called a staff meeting in 1990, there was no pleasure to be had. The meeting took place at the company's Bournemouth factory just before Christmas. With Britain's unemployment rate rising fast, the 340 workers were told that half were to lose their jobs.

There was only one thing more remarkable than the fact that profitable DeVilbiss, the world's leading manufacturer of paint spray guns, was not being forced to make people redundant. "Things were not drastic," says Anderson. "We could have gone on for another five years." What Anderson asked for was perhaps the most extreme partnership with people ever requested: he asked the workers to work with him to achieve the drastic cutback. And they did.

Anderson had joined the company less than 18 months before (just before the Chicago toolmaker ITW bought it), having made himself redundant as production director of Gilbarco in Havant, Hampshire, by recommending that its petrol pump equipment-making operations be consolidated in Essex.

There were no protests, no insults nor any strike threats at the meeting. "You achieve results by soft words," says Anderson. He quietly laid down the proposition that ITW DeVilbiss might be unique in many ways, but it still made a mature product and was threatened in the long term – not only by cheap labour imports, but by competitors who did things in a different and strikingly more efficient way. "To survive," he says, "such companies have agility. We have to go to the very heart of our business to release the maximum potential of our people."

He explained that, if ITW DeVilbiss was to be thus repositioned, it had to stop operating in a functional way (in which people did set jobs). Instead, it needed to start working in a process-dedicated fashion (in which non-specialists worked in multi-disciplinary teams). The Amalgated Union of Engineering Workers cooperated and Anderson hired outplacement specialists to help displaced workers into other careers. "We did it while we could afford it," he says. "That was important. I now speak to other companies that have often left it too late."

ITW DeVilbiss workers have since formed 16 cells, or mini-businesses, which undertake not just production, but the whole process of accepting orders, arranging delivery and even ensuring payment. Previously, orders had gone through 30 different stages. This number was cut dramatically; as were the number of ancillary jobs, such as secretaries, personnel officers, invoice clerks and even many managerial posts. Complex procedures were replaced by simple systems, often using no more than sticky labels carrying all the order requirements. With memos banned, paperwork has been cut by 80 per cent.

They adopted the Japanese Kanban (just in time) system of trays for parts. When empty, more parts have to be ordered. Components have been reduced from 35,000 to 3,700 and suppliers have been cut from 600 to 100; but are paid within seven to 15 days. "When they said they were going to introduce all these new management ideas," says Clive Hughes, deputy team-leader in the aircap cell, "I knew it couldn't happen. I'd been a manager in industry all my life before being made redundant.

"And I was wrong! This is brilliant. It's so easy. Everybody in the cell wants to run "our business" in a really special way. We control budgets, spending £350 at a time without having to ask. Which other workers can do that? Management never bears down on you, demanding to know why you haven't performed. We know our targets because we set them and we know the consequences of not meeting them. It's great. I love it." Anderson continues: "Our people are masters of their own destiny. With that comes ownership, pride and trust. The shopfloor used to have a high staff turnover. But I doubt we've lost three people since going cellular."

Has it all succeeded for ITW DeVilbiss? "We were quoting six to eight weeks to fulfil orders and succeeding 40 per cent of the time," says general manager Barry Holt. "Now we quote 48 hours and succeed 98 per cent." And, adds Anderson: "We're shipping more than 20 per cent more product with less than half the people."

Anderson himself has a new job. ITW has appointed him as worldwide operations specialist, with a brief to introduce his cellular methods to other companies in its 400-strong group.

# Chapter 11

# Employment beyond 2010

Richard Scase, visiting professor at the University of
Essex, writing on behalf of the Economic & Social
Research Council, highlights a number of changes which
will increasingly affect the way businesses operate

In the past the practice was for companies to function as internally
integrated systems – creating structures, functions and tasks as
they grew that managed all of their activities "in house". This
enabled the directors to keep a tight control over these various
activities and was most often undertaken through the application
of the principles of hierarchical line management. According to
these, managers gave orders and workers dutifully executed them.
A culture of compliance predominated and the organisation,
with the aim to function as a well-oiled machine, operated by
reference to precisely-stipulated job descriptions.

## INEFFICIENCY EXISTS EVEN IN RATIONAL MACHINES

To some extent, the above model is something of an exaggeration.
Very few companies operate as rational machines. But the paradigm
is well known and many medium-sized businesses try to function
in this way. However, what is neglected in this model are the
hidden inefficiencies that exist in organisations that attempt to
imitate the model. It is the growing recognition of these that is
bringing about a core re-think about how businesses should
operate and, with this, a reappraisal of the role of management.
The outcome is the emergence of new organisational forms that
will have repercussions for the future nature of work and
employee skills. Traditional forms of organisation are becoming
redundant because the future business will not be a manufacturing

# A valuable ally for policymakers, businesses and other agencies

The ESRC is the UK's largest independent funder of research into economic and social issues. We invest in leading researchers in academic institutions and policy research institutes throughout the UK and provide a gateway to quality research which helps shape public policies and also aids business effectiveness. Our research covers a wide range of issues from national economic performance to the operation of individual firms. It can help you by being more informed about the wider world and of developments which impinge directly on your markets, suppliers and employees.

For further information about the work of the Economic and Social Research Council and how it can help you, please contact the address below.

Or visit our web site: http://www.esrc.ac.uk to find out more about our research centres and programmes, individual projects and publications.

External Relations Division
Economic and Social Research Council
Polaris House
North Star Avenue
Swindon  SN2 1UJ
Tel: 01793 413122  Fax: 01793 413130
E.mail: exrel@esrc.ac.uk

E·S·R·C
ECONOMIC
& SOCIAL
RESEARCH
COUNCIL

enterprise. By the year 2010, only about ten per cent of the labour force will be engaged in manufacturing.

## THE INFORMATION ECONOMY

The next century will witness the continuing growth of the information economy, with businesses trading on the basis of various value-added services that they can provide. This means that their key asset is intellectual capital and not, as in the past, machinery and the capacity to produce standardised products for either high volume or niche markets (as is the case for large numbers of small and medium-sized enterprises).

Intellectual capital refers to the knowledge that a company possesses to be innovative in continuously developing new products and services that are relevant for gaining competitive advantage in their targeted markets. In other words, in an information economy, intellectual capital is the basis for a company's core competencies. Everything else that may have been undertaken within traditional, highly integrated enterprises can now be outsourced, often on a global basis. The key challenge for businesses in Britain at the start of the 21st century is to nurture creativity and innovation. It is the ability to do this that will differentiate successful, high-performing, and competitive businesses from the rest.

How can creativity be nurtured in businesses so that there is continuous innovation? In many ways, there are lessons to be learned from the ways in which many small and medium-sized enterprises operate. Those of them that are high-performing have a clarity of vision. The founding owners have a clear idea of where they want their businesses to go. But an additional and vital ingredient is that so do their employees. In other words, there is an employer-employee partnership in which the vision is shared. To implement this simple principle, however, requires the presence of a range of organisational features:

- *That there is open, honest and fluid communication around all matters that are likely to affect the company's future;*

- *This, in turn, demands the existence of a culture of high trust between employers and employees;*

- *This in itself requires that employees are trained and given the capacity to develop their own talents for their own self development as well as for the good of the enterprise. They must feel themselves as stakeholders, participating in the rewards of the company as it grows. This can be in a variety of forms ranging from equity stakes (as in many business partnerships) to profit sharing and career prospects.*

It is within such organisational contexts that creativity is nurtured. These features account for the rapid growth of many small and medium-sized firms in such diverse industries as high technology, bioscience, professional services, advertising and entertainment. Often such organisational attributes are structured around the "charisma" or the personalities of the founder-owners. Although this can be an advantage, it is not an absolute necessity. But what is vital for high performance is continuous innovation by leveraging the creativity of employees through developing these organisational processes mentioned above.

Product innovation through employee creativity requires a redefined psychological contract between employer and employee. It demands a shift from compliance to internalised commitment. Essentially, this means that employees are excited by their jobs – they eat, sleep and drink their work. Their jobs are at the heart of their personal identities and inherent to their notions of self. Again, it is only through managing the business as a partnership between employers and employees that this can be achieved. This can often have ramifications for the design and location of businesses.

If, in the past, the workplace was the place where work was done, in the information economy it is the place where ideas are exchanged and problems solved. This normally requires close working relationships among colleagues and the cultivation of positive team dynamics. It not only places a premium on selecting potential employees who are technically competent, but also on recruiting people who are personally compatible with others in the business. It also means the architecture and the design of the workplace needs to facilitate this process.

## THE CREATIVE ENVIRONMENT

What is striking about businesses that compete on the basis of their intellectual capital is how they convey the physical impression that nothing much is being produced. This is because the workplace is designed to encourage face-to-face encounters among colleagues for the purposes of problem-solving and for the generation of new ideas. This means that a high proportion of floor space is designated as "public areas", consisting of comfortable sofas arranged around vending machines. These areas are the nerve centres of creative businesses. Through discussion in these areas, colleagues develop ideas and then return to their "private spheres" (and this is increasingly at home instead of at the workplace) to explore further the potential and feasibility. These thoughts will then be fed back to colleagues in the coffee area on a later occasion.

A significant feature of this is that the innovative process is not formally structured. It is not a specialist or compartmentalised activity as is often the case in traditional manufacturing companies. Instead, it is located at the very heart of the business process and is essentially informal and unstructured. Employers cannot tell employees to be creative. Intellectual capital does not operate in this way. But what employers can do is to provide the organisational and architectural contexts which facilitate employee creativity and then to reward employees so that they have a stakeholder interest in the innovative outcomes. This often means more than simply material rewards. It can be part-ownership of patents, as in bioscience, or the opportunity for professional recognition, as in the entertainment industry.

Location is also an important factor for leveraging creativity and fully utilising the intellectual capital of a business. Why is it that the centre of the global entertainment industry continues to be located in congested Los Angeles? Why do advertising agencies locate in parts of London and software companies in the Thames valley? It is because these geographical areas constitute clusters of tacit knowledge, of intellectual skills from which all firms benefit. Pools of talent become geographically concentrated which then shape the character of local infrastructures. In this way, local labour markets from which companies recruit consist of pools of the appropriate intellectual capital. In many ways these are similar to the industrial districts of the early Industrial Revolution. In these, cultures became established which enhanced the capabilities of each of the separate businesses.

## THE LIMITS OF A VIRTUAL WORKPLACE

This is why there are limits to the extent to which information technology can completely abolish the need for the workplace. A barrier to the adoption of the virtual organisation, as enabled by the capabilities of information technology, is the need for those with intellectual capital to interface in spontaneous and unstructured ways. It is through such means that creativity can be leveraged for the development of innovative products and services. In order for companies to be competitive in the information economy, they need to re-design their operational processes, management styles and compliant cultures. This will require self-confident leadership in which openness and informality are encouraged. The design and architecture of their workplaces will need to embody these assumptions. Businesses will need to function as partnerships in all of their aspects, from strategic decision-making to the structuring of reward systems. Without these mechanisms in place, intellectual capital – as the core asset of information-based businesses – will simply walk out of the door. Unlike machinery in factories, people – especially those with creative knowledge – cannot be bolted to the floor.

*The ESRC is launching a new programme called the Future of Work which will analyse trends in employment and work beyond the Millennium. For more information see page 80.*

# Where do we go from here?

**If you think that your company can improve the way its people are managed and, as a result, significantly improve its performance, the following pages contain some useful help and advice on where to start. Work through the steps below and use the Partnerships with People questionnaire and checklist to identify where you are presently and to chart your future course**

The following are key steps that outstanding organisations have taken to make "people partnerships" really work and turn the words into action:

**1** *Use the Partnerships with People questionnaire and checklist to determine where your company is now.*

**2** *Re-run the exercise from time to time to ensure that the company remains on course and that all employees agree that objectives have been met.*

**3** *Use this guide and the powerful findings of the* Partnerships with people *report to stimulate discussion between you and your senior colleagues, in order to determine in which areas you might look to improve the way you manage your people.*

**4** *Ensure that you all genuinely believe that people do make the critical difference and that you are all personally committed to driving the change programme throughout the business.*

**5** *Be prepared for a long, hard road that is likely to stretch your patience, endurance and enthusiasm to the limit, but that will be well worth it in the end!*

**6** *Progressively involve all your people in the process, so that everyone is pulling in the same direction and feels part of it.*

**7** *Find out at a very early stage what your people honestly think about you and the company. This can be done through a non-threatening Independent Attitudes Survey, that will highlight the areas of real concern.*

**8** *Listen to what your people tell you in the survey and act promptly to get some early wins to provide vital momentum and inspire confidence that you really mean what you say.*

**9** *Make use of appropriate support organisations including those featured in this Guide and in the* Partnerships with people *report. And, if you have not already done so, take a look at change tools such as Investors in People, the Business Excellence Model and the Making training Pay toolkit, etc. to assist in the implementation of your change programme.*

**10** *Identify other companies seeking to bring the best out of their people and share your learning and both good and bad experiences with them on a regular basis to mutual benefit.*

You will have really made it, when your people use these words to describe your business: "People are proud to work here, proud of colleagues, proud of the company and proud of themselves."

## THE PARTNERSHIPS WITH PEOPLE CHECKPOINT

The main points of the Five Paths to Success (as outlined in Chapter 1), have been compressed into a single framework below. Using this as a reference, you can work through the questionnaire overleaf to assess your organisation.

| | STAGE 1 — Starting out | STAGE 2 — Moving forward | STAGE 3 — New horizons |
|---|---|---|---|
| **SHARED GOALS** — Understanding the business we are in | ■ Plan developed from the MD's vision<br>■ The plan explained to all staff<br>■ Performance against plan is shared | ■ The vision developed by top team<br>■ The vision shared with all the people<br>■ Jobs related to the longer-term goals | ■ Participative planning enabled<br>■ Unit planning facilitated<br>■ Agile planning operated |
| **SHARED CULTURE** — Agreed values that bind us together | ■ Managers are fair and involved<br>■ Commitment to your customers<br>■ Start to tackle the fear of change | ■ Build collective confidence<br>■ Demonstrate you value everyone<br>■ Face problems – be tough | ■ Lessons are learned, blame is removed<br>■ Shape a competitive culture<br>■ Change is embraced |
| **SHARED LEARNING** — Continuously improving ourselves | ■ Performance measures are defined<br>■ Employees are trained for job competence<br>■ Recruit and select with care | ■ People enrolled in their own development<br>■ Managers are developed to achieve stretching targets<br>■ High performance is expected | ■ Develop the person<br>■ Train managers as coaches<br>■ Build tomorrow's capability |
| **SHARED EFFORT** — One business driven by flexible teams | ■ Managers developed as team leaders<br>■ Team performance measured<br>■ Team problem-solving encouraged | ■ Teams trained as effective working units<br>■ Discretion given to teams<br>■ Teams made internal customers | ■ Inter-team working required<br>■ Ad hoc teams used<br>■ Build the firm as 'the team' |
| **SHARED INFORMATION** — Effective communication throughout the enterprise | ■ Communications effectiveness is checked<br>■ Process for reporting decisions is used<br>■ Communicate through behaviour | ■ Be open; good and bad news is relayed<br>■ Process in place to allow ideas to be taken into account<br>■ Information is shared between teams | ■ Information is available to allow decisions to be delegated<br>■ Everyone is responsible for seeking and passing on information |

# THE PARTNERSHIPS WITH PEOPLE QUESTIONNAIRE

There are 15 questions below – three for each of the Five Paths to Success outlined in the Partnerships with people report. Once you have read each question, circle the most appropriate response.

0: to no extent; 1: to a little extent; 2: to a slight extent; 3: to a moderate extent; 4: to a great extent; 5: to a very great extent

## TO WHAT EXTENT...

### PATH 1

|  | | | | | | |
|---|---|---|---|---|---|---|
| ...is there a step-by-step plan to develop the business which all employees fully understand? | 0 | 1 | 2 | 3 | 4 | 5 |
| ...do all staff contribute creative ideas about how objectives can be implemented? | 0 | 1 | 2 | 3 | 4 | 5 |
| ...is the firm's strategy and business plan widely discussed before it is agreed? | 0 | 1 | 2 | 3 | 4 | 5 |
| PATH 1 TOTAL SCORE | | | | | | |

### PATH 2

| Question | | | | | | |
|---|---|---|---|---|---|---|
| ...would all employees say "managers are fair and respect every employee"? | 0 | 1 | 2 | 3 | 4 | 5 |
| ...do both staff and managers expect that every employee will be dedicated and professional? | 0 | 1 | 2 | 3 | 4 | 5 |
| ...does the culture of the firm develop widespread confidence and a 'can do' attitude? | 0 | 1 | 2 | 3 | 4 | 5 |
| PATH 2 TOTAL SCORE | | | | | | |

### PATH 3

| Question | | | | | | |
|---|---|---|---|---|---|---|
| ...is everyone highly skilled to perform their tasks? | 0 | 1 | 2 | 3 | 4 | 5 |
| ...does everyone feel that they are developing new knowledge and skills? | 0 | 1 | 2 | 3 | 4 | 5 |
| ...are people being deliberately developed to provide a competitive advantage for the firm? | 0 | 1 | 2 | 3 | 4 | 5 |
| PATH 3 TOTAL SCORE | | | | | | |

### PATH 4

| Question | | | | | | |
|---|---|---|---|---|---|---|
| ...do staff (at every level) work in high-performing teams? | 0 | 1 | 2 | 3 | 4 | 5 |
| ...are there efficient mechanisms to ensure that teams co-operate? | 0 | 1 | 2 | 3 | 4 | 5 |
| ...do teams form and re-form to solve problems quickly and efficiently? | 0 | 1 | 2 | 3 | 4 | 5 |
| PATH 4 TOTAL SCORE | | | | | | |

### PATH 5

| Question | | | | | | |
|---|---|---|---|---|---|---|
| ...is there a frequent and open cascade of communication down the organisation? | 0 | 1 | 2 | 3 | 4 | 5 |
| ...is there continuous and open communication across the organisation? | 0 | 1 | 2 | 3 | 4 | 5 |
| ...is there comprehensive and open communication flowing up the organisation – so that top management really knows what is going on? | 0 | 1 | 2 | 3 | 4 | 5 |
| PATH 5 TOTAL SCORE | | | | | | |

## HOW DOES YOUR ORGANISATION RATE?

Use the chart below to add up your totals.

| | STAGE 1 Starting out | | | | | STAGE 2 Moving forward | | | | | STAGE 3 New horizons | | | | |
|---|---|---|---|---|---|---|---|---|---|---|---|---|---|---|---|
| Path score | 1 | 2 | 3 | 4 | 5 | 6 | 7 | 8 | 9 | 10 | 11 | 12 | 13 | 14 | 15 |
| **PATH 1** Shared goals | | | | | | | | | | | | | | | |
| **PATH 2** Shared culture | | | | | | | | | | | | | | | |
| **PATH 3** Shared learning | | | | | | | | | | | | | | | |
| **PATH 4** Shared effort | | | | | | | | | | | | | | | |
| **PATH 5** Shared information | | | | | | | | | | | | | | | |

## SELF-ASSESSMENT MAPPING GRID

**The map you have drawn using the Partnerships with People questionnaire and checklist represents the profile of your company in relation to the way that it is perceived by its most valuable resource – your employees**

If you have a score of less than three for any of the paths, that path needs to be worked on first to bring the organisation up to Stage 1 (starting out) status. After a suitable period of time, re-run the questionnaire to assess whether there is company-wide agreement that this has been achieved.

A company will not benefit from going along one path to the exclusion of others. A broad approach to all paths will balance the organisation and bring the greatest results and rewards.

An interesting exercise is for senior executives, middle managers and shopfloor employees to work through the questionnaire independently of each other, adding up the scores in the grid on page 77. A number of companies that have already conducted this exercise have seen very different sets of answers from each of these groups.

## SOME USEFUL SOURCES OF INFORMATION

### ORGANISATIONS

■ DTI Innovation Unit          Tel: 0171 215 1994
151 Buckingham Palace Road     Fax: 0171 215 1997
London
SW1W 9SS

■ Institute of Personnel and Development  Tel: 0181 971 9000
IPD House                      Fax: 0181 263 3355
35 Camp Road
London
SW19 4UX

■ Investors in People UK        Tel: 0171 467 1900
7-10 Chandos Street            Fax: 0171 636 2386
London
W1M 9DE

■ British Quality Foundation    Tel: 0171 654 5000
32-34 Great Peter Street       Fax: 0171 654 5001
London
SW1P 2QX

■ Economic and Social Research Council  Tel: 01793 413000
Polaris House                  Fax: 01793 413001
North Star Avenue
Swindon
SN2 1UJ

### PUBLICATIONS AND PRODUCTS AVAILABLE

■ Department of Trade and Industry

The *Partnerships with People* report is available free from the DTI, Admail, 528, London SW1W 8YT or use the orderline (tel: 0870 150 2500; fax: 0870 150 2333).

For up-to-date information on all aspects of DTI Innovation activities, contact the Innovation Unit (tel: 0171 215 1994).

Management Best Practice Information and Services can be accessed on www.dti.gov.uk/mbp. For more information on the Inside UK Enterprise Scheme, contact 01730 235015.

Information on the UK Benchmarking Index is available from your local Business Link. The contact number for England is 0345 567765. In Wales, telephone 0345 969798 and in Scotland 0141 248 4774.

- Institute of Personnel and Development

  To receive a copy of the IPD publications catalogue or for information on products such as the *Making training pay* toolkit (price £44.00), contact: Institute of Personnel and Development (tel: 0181 263 3387 or e-mail publish@ipd.co.uk).

- Investors in People UK

  The following toolkits are available:
  *Building a better business* (price £65.00)
  *Making training pay* (price £44.00)
  *Achieving excellence through people* (price £95.00)

  Investors in People UK also produces a comprehensive range of publications. For more details about products and publications, contact: Investors in People UK, PO Box 242, Goldthorpe, Rotherham, S63 9YP. (tel: 01709 892782; fax: 01709 892783). A charge of £6.00 will be added to all orders for p&p.

- British Quality Foundation

  More information on the Business Excellence Model, ASSESS and other products and services is available from the British Quality Foundation. (tel: 0171 654 5000; fax: 0171 654 5001).

- Economic & Social Research Council

  The ESRC is launching a new programme on the Future of Work which will analyse trends in employment and work beyond the Millennium. For further details, contact ESRC External Relations (tel: 01793 413122; fax: 01793 413130).

*Colour* **Aids**

# ediatrics

**n Thomas** MRCP
nt Paediatrician
k Park Hospital
JK

**Harvey** FRCP DCH
nt Paediatrician
arlotte's Maternity Hospital
JK

Cl    ill Livingstone

EDI    LONDON MELBOURNE AND N

CHURCHILL LIVINGSTONE
Medical Division of Longman Group Limited

Distributed in the United States of America by
Churchill Livingstone Inc., 1560 Broadway, New York,
N.Y. 10036, and by associated companies, branches
and representatives throughout the world

First published 1986

ISBN 0 443 029733

British Library Cataloguing in Publication Data

Thomas, Roslyn
    Paediatrics.—(Colour aids)
    1. Children—Diseases—Atlases
    I. Title  II. Harvey, David, 1936–     III. Series
    618.92'00022'      RJ48.5

Library of Congress Cataloging in Publication Data

Thomas, Roslyn.
    Paediatrics.
    (Colour aids)
    1. Pediatrics—Atlases.  2. Children—Diseases—
    Atlases.  I. Harvey, David (David Robert)  II. Title.
    III. Series.  [DNLM; 1. Pediatrics—atlases.
    WS 17 T461p]
    RJ48.5.T48  1986      618.92      85-21358

Produced by Longman Group (FE) Ltd
Printed in Hong Kong

# Contents

# Acknowledgement

We thank Diana Woo for allowing us to use the cover photograph of herself and her daughter.

London, 1986                                                  R.T.
                                                                        D.H.

# Developmental Milestones (1)

## Birth to 6 weeks

**Gross motor**

At birth there is marked head lag when the infant is pulled from the supine position (Fig. 1). In ventral suspension with the examiner's hand supporting the chest (Fig. 3) the back is rounded, and there is some flexion of the hips and knees. By 6 weeks of age the infant can lift his head when placed in the prone position (Fig. 2) and there is some head control when pulled from supine to sitting.

**Fine motor and vision**

A baby can see at birth, but by 6 weeks can fix his vision on objects and will follow horizontally across to 90 degrees.

**Hearing and speech**

Response to noise will be indicated by startle or quietening to a soothing voice.

**Social behaviour**

The infant will stop crying when picked up to be nursed. He also begins to smile in response to familiar noises and faces by five weeks.

**Fig. 1** Head lag.

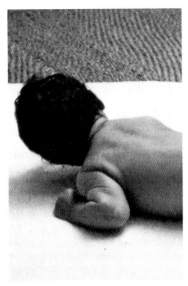

**Fig. 2** Lifting head when prone — by 6 weeks.

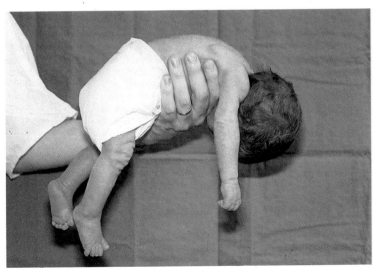

**Fig. 3** Ventral suspension showing rounded back.

# Developmental Milestones (2)

## 3–6 months

**Gross motor**

By 6 months the infant in the prone position kicks well, pushes up from his forearms, lifting his head and chest (Fig. 4), and begins to roll from front to back. He can sit with support or leaning forward into the tripod position (Fig. 5). The age of first sitting alone ranges from 4½–8½ months. He begins to weight-bear and to rise to the standing position when supported by the arms or chest.

**Fine motor and vision**

The infant will reach out for objects with a coarse palmar approach and will clasp and retain small objects placed in his hand. He places objects into his mouth and also begins to release objects.

**Hearing and speech**

The infant can laugh, gurgle and coo. Around 6 months he usually begins to babble. He will turn when his name is called.

**Social behaviour**

The infant holds on to his bottle or feeding cup when fed and frolics when played with. He examines and plays with his own hands and places the feet into his mouth (Fig. 6).

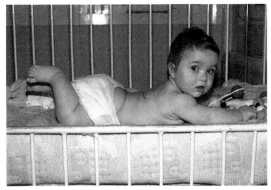

**Fig. 4** A press-up at 6 months.

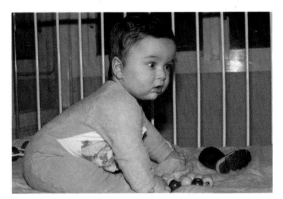

**Fig. 5** Sitting in tripod position.

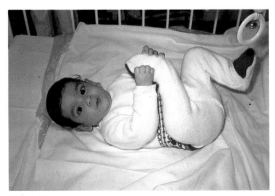

**Fig. 6** Playing with feet.

## 1 | Developmental Milestones (3)

### 6–9 months

**Gross motor**

By 6 months, the infant can roll from front to back. He sits unsupported with a straight back (Fig. 7). He begins to pivot around on his arms and legs into the crawling position (Fig. 9). He may also begin to crawl on hands and knees.

**Fine motor and vision**

Small objects are picked up between index finger and thumb in a pincer grasp. Objects are transferred from one hand to the other (Fig. 8).

**Hearing and speech**

By 9 months he shouts to gain attention and vocalises non-specific syllables such as 'dada' and 'mama'.

**Social behaviour**

The baby turns when being talked to and resists when objects are taken from him. He tries to reach objects out of his reach. He likes to feed himself with his fingers.

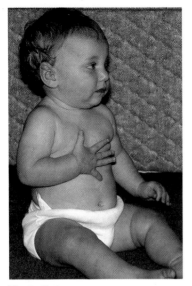

**Fig. 7** Sitting unsupported.

**Fig. 8** Transferring objects.

**Fig. 9** Getting into a crawling position.

# 1 | Developmental Milestones (4)

## 9–12 months

**Gross motor**

Most infants are crawling by 9–10 months of age. About 10% of normal infants never crawl, but move around by rolling, paddling, or bottom shuffling (Fig. 10). Such children are often late walkers, and other family members may have also exhibited this normal variant of motor development. These children may not walk alone until 2 years of age. The child of 9–12 months begins to pull himself to standing (Fig. 11) and to cruise around the room holding on to furniture.

**Fine motor and vision**

The infant will bang two cubes together. He also looks for fallen objects.

**Hearing and speech**

By 9–12 months he usually has one or two recognisable single words in addition to 'mama' and 'dada'.

**Social behaviour**

He enjoys imitative games such as clapping hands and waving goodbye, but is shy with strangers until the end of his first year.

**Fig. 10** Normal variant of getting around.

**Fig. 11** Getting up to standing.

# Developmental Milestones (5)

## 12–18 months

**Gross motor**

By 12 months, the child can usually walk with his hands held (Fig. 12) and he begins to stand alone. Only 3% have not begun to walk by 18 months of age. At that time, the child will be climbing onto chairs and up stairs. He will also hold on to toys while walking.

**Fine motor and vision**

The pincer grip becomes more refined and tiny objects can be picked up delicately (Fig. 13). The child also points at objects with his index finger (Fig. 14). He casts objects down repeatedly and can be persuaded to give objects to another person on request. He builds a tower with two or three bricks.

**Hearing and speech**

There is a vocabulary of several words and the child usually also repeats his own name. Comprehension is more advanced than speech at this age. He enjoys looking at pictures in a book and often points and babbles while doing this.

**Social behaviour**

By 12 months, the child indicates his wants, usually by pointing. He drinks from a cup and helps to feed himself. He also begins to help with dressing. The child learns to throw and enjoys simple games such as peek-a-boo (Fig. 15).

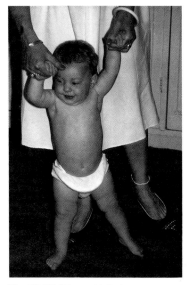

**Fig. 12** Walking with help.

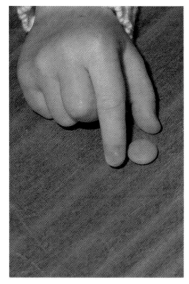

**Fig. 13** Pincer grip.

**Fig. 14** Pointing.

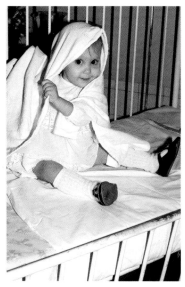

**Fig. 15** Peek-a-boo.

# 2 | Nutrition and Growth (1)

## Normal growth

Growth in childhood is influenced by genetic, nutritional and emotional factors as well as specific diseases and hormonal deficiencies. Accurate measurements of height (Figs 16, 18), weight and head circumference should be plotted on centile charts throughout childhood.

**Height and weight**

Growth in infancy is rapid. This is followed by slow steady growth in middle childhood until the adolescent growth spurt after which final adult height is reached and epiphyseal fusion takes place. The growth of most children follows a course similar to those of the centile charts. Height below the third centile occurs in 3% of normal healthy children and their parents' height should also be measured in order to assess whether such children have genetic short stature or a disorder of growth. The majority of preterm and small-for-gestational-age infants achieve normal adult size, unless there is very severe intrauterine growth retardation.

**Head growth**

The major postnatal growth in brain and head circumference occurs in the first 3 years of life. Asymmetry of the skull (plagiocephaly) and face (Fig. 17) caused by intrauterine posture is common in infancy and usually improves with age. Premature fusion of the skull sutures (craniosynostosis) occasionally results in asymmetry of the skull.

**Fig. 16** Accurate measurement of height.

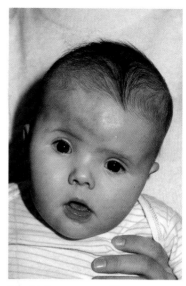

**Fig. 17** Asymmetry of face and skull.

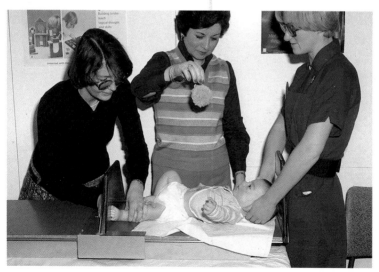

**Fig. 18** Measurement of height.

# 2 | Nutrition and Growth (2)

## Short stature

**Aetiology**

Most short children are normal and have short parents. Others may have chromosomal abnormalities such as Turner's syndrome, primary or secondary hypopituitarism, hypothyroidism, isolated growth hormone deficiency, chondrodysplasia, or iatrogenic causes (particularly long-term corticosteroid therapy).

**Clinical features and investigation**

Physical examination usually reveals other dysmorphic features in chromosomal abnormalities and chondrodysplasias. In chondrodysplasia there are usually disproportionately short limbs or trunk (Fig. 19) and skeletal X-rays are abnormal. Juvenile hypothyroidism results in progressive growth failure (Fig. 20), severe retardation of bone age, coarse facies (Fig. 21) and intellectual retardation. In isolated growth hormone deficiency, the child is usually over-weight for his height. Serial height measurements show reduced growth velocity and stimulation tests of pituitary function demonstrate specific failure of growth hormone production. Multiple pituitary hormone failure is usually secondary to neoplasia (particularly craniopharyngioma), radiotherapy or trauma.

**Management**

Depends on underlying cause. If a hormonal deficiency is found, specific replacement therapy is indicated. Catch-up growth and height depend on the age at diagnosis and the duration and severity of the underlying disorder.

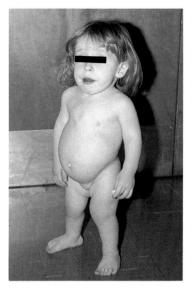

**Fig. 19** Short-limbed chondrodysplasia. (By courtesy of Dr G. Supramanian.)

**Fig. 20** 16-year-old boy with short stature due to hypothyroidism with a normal 16-year-old.

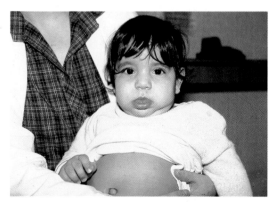

**Fig. 21** Coarse facies in juvenile hypothyroidism.

| # Nutrition and Growth (3)

## Failure to thrive

**Definition**

Failure to gain weight at the normal rate in early childhood. Birth weight is normal, but normal weight gain does not occur. If the underlying cause of the problem is not resolved for some time, height and head circumference may also be affected.

**Aetiology**

The most common cause is inadequate dietary intake. Congenital malformations, chromosomal disorders and specific syndromes can usually be diagnosed or suspected on routine physical examination. The commonest causes of malabsorption in childhood are cystic fibrosis and coeliac disease.

**Clinical features**

The weight chart will show progressive deviation from the normal. The buttocks are thin and wasted (Fig. 22), and there is loss of subcutaneous fat with poor muscle bulk (Fig. 23). If failure to thrive is caused by malabsorption, abdominal distension (Fig. 24) is common and rickets occasionally occurs.

**Investigation**

Dietary intake must be assessed. Anaemia and steatorrhoea are suggestive of malabsorption. Sweat test and jejunal biopsy will make the diagnoses of cystic fibrosis and coeliac disease respectively.

## Obesity

**Aetiology**

Common health problem in Western society; rarely caused by endocrine disturbance. Often has a genetic component.

**Clinical features**

Weight is greater than expected from height centile even though they are often quite tall. Skin fold thickness is excessive.

**Management**

Prevention or early change in dietary habit is desirable, as established obesity is very difficult to treat.

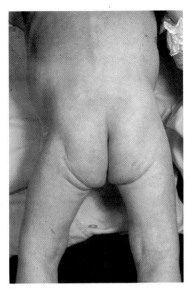

**Fig. 22** Wasted buttocks in coeliac disease.

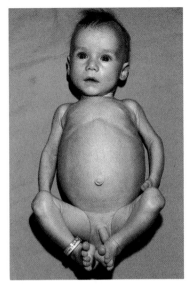

**Fig. 23** Failure to thrive with distended abdomen and wasted limbs.

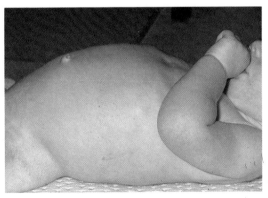

**Fig. 24** Abdominal distension in coeliac disease.

## Malnutrition

**Clinical features**

*Marasmus*
Severe generalised under-nutrition. In developing countries it is usually due to failure to breast feed and inadequate dietary intake. Sometimes occurs in chronic illness. Extreme emaciation (Fig. 25) and increased susceptibility to gastroenteritis and infection are common.

*Protein energy malnutrition (kwashiorkor)*
Inadequate dietary protein intake resulting in oedema (Fig. 26), cheilosis (Fig. 27), and depigmented and scaly skin, and sparse friable reddish hair (Fig. 28). The infant usually has a poor appetite and is listless and irritable. Fatty infiltration of the liver causes hepatomegaly.

**Prevention**

Community health education should aim to prevent nutritional deficiency states. Breast feeding should be encouraged, particularly in developing countries where formula milks are often expensive. Cheap nutritious local foods should be introduced into the infant's diet from 4–6 months of age.

**Management**

Early recognition of deficiency states and gradual reintroduction of an adequate local diet. Associated infections may require treatment, and vitamin supplementation is usually necessary.

PAEDIATRICS

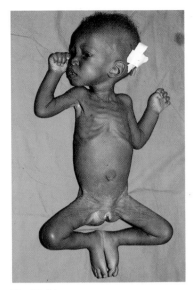

**Fig. 25** Marasmus.

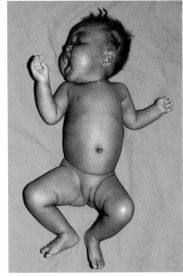

**Fig. 26** Protein energy malnutrition (PEM or kwashiorkor).

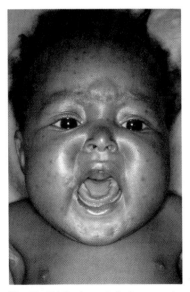

**Fig. 27** Cheilosis and depigmented skin in PEM.

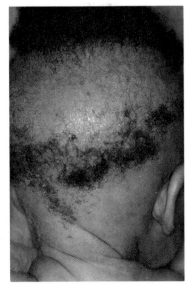

**Fig. 28** Sparse friable hair in PEM.

# 2 | Nutrition and Growth (5)

## Rickets

**Aetiology**

The most common cause is vitamin D deficiency due to inadequate dietary intake. Malabsorption, liver disease, renal failure, renal tubular dysfunction, and long-term anticonvulsant therapy may also cause rickets.

**Clinical features**

Swelling of long bone metaphyses particularly at the wrist (Fig. 29), bowing of the legs, chest deformity, rachitic rosary (Fig. 30). Craniotabes and delayed closure of the fontanelle may occur in young infants. The child is often irritable and fretful and has bone tenderness and muscle weakness.

**Diagnosis**

The classical biochemical disturbance is hypocalcaemia, hypophosphataemia and vitamin D deficiency accompanied by a raised bone alkaline phosphatase level. Radiological signs of rickets include splaying of the metaphyses of long bones with delayed ossification of the epiphyses. Pathological fractures and deformity of weight-bearing long bones sometimes occur.

**Management**

Vitamin D supplementation and improved dietary intake. High dosage may be necessary in renal rickets or hereditary hypophosphataemic rickets.

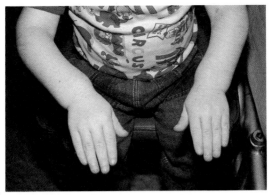

**Fig. 29** Swelling of metaphyses at wrists.

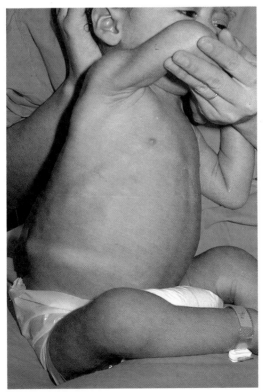

**Fig. 30** Rachitic rosary.

# 3 | Endocrine Disorders (1)

## Adrenogenital syndrome

**Synonyms** Congenital adrenal hyperplasia (CAH).

**Incidence** 1 in 5000 live births.

**Aetiology** Autosomal recessive disorder due to enzyme deficiency in cortisol and aldosterone synthesis resulting in excessive testosterone production. The commonest type is due to 21-hydroxylase deficiency.

**Clinical features** Affected females are virilised from birth (Fig. 31) and may be confused for males with severe hypospadias and bilateral cryptorchidism. If virilisation is not recognised early, particularly in male infants, they may collapse in the second week of life with a life-threatening adrenal crisis.

**Diagnosis** Elevated plasma 17-hydroxyprogesterone level, plasma ACTH and urinary steroid excretion.

**Management** Salt-losing crises require urgent resuscitation with intravenous saline. Replacement hydrocortisone and a salt-retaining steroid, fludrocortisone, are required for long-term suppression of the hyperplastic adrenal glands.

## Cushing's syndrome

**Aetiology** Excessive cortisol production usually due to bilateral adrenal hyperplasia caused by pituitary adenomata; occasionally caused by local adrenal adenoma or carcinoma. High dosage administration of corticosteroids will produce similar clinical features.

**Clinical features** Moon facies (Fig. 32), truncal obesity, hirsutism acne, striae (Fig. 33), growth retardation, osteoporosis and muscle wasting.

**Management** Surgery with or without radiotherapy.

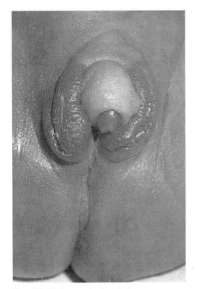

**Fig. 31** Enlarged clitoris in adrenogenital syndrome.

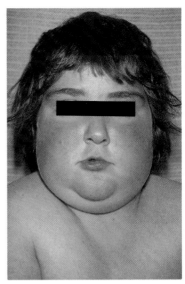

**Fig. 32** Moon facies in Cushing's syndrome.

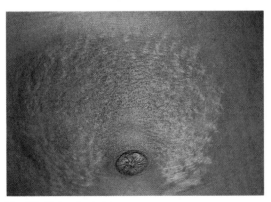

**Fig. 33** Abdominal striae.

# 3 | Endocrine Disorders (2)

## Precocious puberty

**Definition**

Development of secondary sex characteristics before the age of 8 years in girls and 10 years in boys.

**Incidence**

Early puberty is more common in girls than boys, and isolated premature thelarche (Fig. 34) (breast development) is relatively common.

**Aetiology**

In physiological early puberty, there is premature activation of the hypothalamo-pituitary-gonadal axis. Cerebral tumours, particularly pineal tumours in boys, gonadal or adrenal tumours, and exogenous steroid administration also cause early development of secondary sex characteristics.

**Clinical features and diagnosis**

Careful physical examination may help to distinguish between physiological but early onset of puberty, and pathological development (Figs 35, 36) Discrepancies from the usual sequence of pubertal development, such as pubic hair but no breast development, are unlikely to be physiological. Abdominal palpation and ultrasound are important in the detection of adrenal or gonadal tumours. Intracranial tumours must always be exluded.

**Management**

Pathological causes such as hypothyroidism or tumours require specific treatment. Short stature is the major long-term physical disadvantage of early puberty because of the shorter period of prepubertal growth before epiphyseal fusion. Early puberty is also psychologically upsetting to both child and parents. Drug therapy may be used to suppress gonadotrophin release until the child reaches an appropriate age.

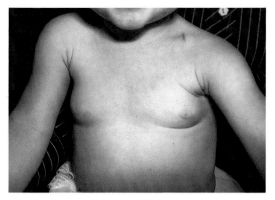

**Fig. 34** Premature breast development.

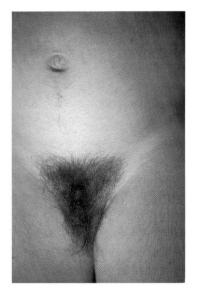

**Fig. 35** Sexual precocity at 5 years of age (adrenal tumour).

**Fig. 36** Pathological enlargement of clitoris.

# 3 | Endocrine Disorders (3)

## Hypothyroidism

**Incidence**

Relatively common; congenital hypothyroidism occurs in 1 in 4000 live births.

**Aetiology**

Congenital hypothyroidism is usually due to thyroid agenesis; occasionally due to inherited dysgenesis of hormone synthesis.

**Clinical features**

Coarse facies (Fig. 37), dry skin, hoarse voice and cry and paucity of spontaneous activity. Hypothermia, hypotonia and poor weight gain are common. Umbilical hernia, constipation and prolonged jaundice sometimes occur in neonates. Intellectual retardation is the major long-term effect in young infants. Some have cerebellar ataxia, myopia and squints. In juvenile hypothyroidism occurring in later childhood there is growth failure but very little intellectual impairment if thyroid function has been normal during the early critical period of brain growth.

**Management**

Replacement therapy (Fig. 38) with L-thyroxine for life. Dosage is adjusted to achieve normal growth and bone age as well as suppression of thyroid stimulating hormone.

## Hyperthyroidism

**Incidence**

Uncommon. Neonatal thyrotoxicosis may occur in infants of mothers with a history of thyrotoxicosis and thyroid stimulating immunoglobulins.

**Clinical features**

Young infants have tachycardia, vomiting, sweating, poor weight gain and irritability. Older children may also have rapid growth, tremor, and proptosis and goitre (Fig. 39).

**Management**

Antithyroid drugs such as carbimazole until spontaneous remission, usually within 2 years. Some require thyroidectomy. Neonatal thyrotoxicosis resolves within a few weeks; sometimes no treatment is needed.

**Fig. 37** Coarse facies in juvenile hypothyroidism.

**Fig. 38** Same boy after 1 year of replacement therapy.

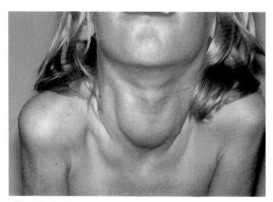

**Fig. 39** Goitre in hyperthyroidism.

# 4 | Infection (1)

## Measles

**Clinical features**

After an incubation period of 10–14 days, there is a prodromal illness with fever, coryza, conjunctivitis and cough. The child is extremely miserable and for about 24 hours before and after the rash appears, tiny white spots on a bright red background (Koplik's spots) may be seen on the buccal mucosa of the cheek. After 3–4 days, a florid, maculopapular rash appears on the face and behind the ears (Fig. 40). The rash becomes more confluent as it spreads down the trunk (Fig. 41); bronzing and desquamation occur after 4–7 days.

**Complications**

Bronchopneumonia and otitis media are common; encephalitis occurs in 1 in 1000 children with measles. Rarely, a slowly progressive neurodegenerative disorder (subacute sclerosing panencephalitis—SSPE) occurs some years after acute measles.

**Immunisation**

Measles carries a high morbidity; mortality is high in chidren with malnutrition or immunodeficiency. Immunisation is recommended at 12–18 months of age.

## German measles (rubella)

**Clinical features**

Incubation period 14–21 days. Mild illness with transient, non-specific pink macular rash lasting only a few days. Generalised lymphadenopathy, particularly with involvement of the suboccipital nodes, is common.

**Complications**

Thrombocytopenia occasionally occurs. Arthritis is more common in adolescent females. Rubella embryopathy affecting the developing fetus in the first trimester of pregnancy is the most devastating complication.

**Immunisation**

All girls should be vaccinated before puberty. In some countries, all children receive rubella immunisation in infancy.

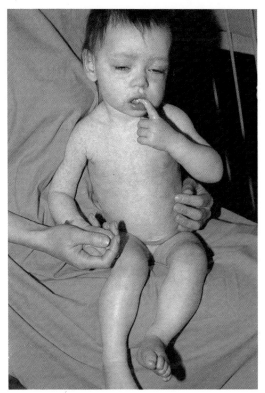

**Fig. 40** Miserable child with measles.

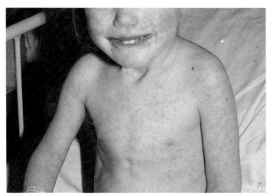

**Fig. 41** Measles rash.

## Mumps

**Clinical features**

Fever and enlargement of one or both parotid glands (Fig. 42) occur 14–21 days after contact by a susceptible individual. Many children have subclinical infection. The brawny, swollen glands are painful, tender and often accompanied by earache or trismus. Submandibular salivary glands may also be affected, and differentiation from lymphadenopathy may occasionally be difficult.

**Complications**

Meningitis is common, but mild. It may precede or occur in the absence of parotid swelling. Pancreatitis and epididymo-orchitis occur more often in adults.

**Immunisation**

Vaccine is available; opinions differ as to whether it is warranted in view of the mild nature of the illness.

## Infectious mononucleosis
### (glandular fever)

**Clinical features**

Sporadic infection caused by the Epstein-Barr virus after an incubation period of 4–14 days. Anorexia, malaise, fever and generalised lymphadenopathy are prominent symptoms. There may be petechiae on the palate, and in children a severe exudative tonsillitis often occurs. A macular rash occurs in approximately 20% of cases, and in 90% if ampicillin is given (Fig. 43).

**Diagnosis**

Atypical mononuclear cells appear in the blood film, and agglutination tests (such as Paul-Bunnell test) may be positive in the early weeks.

**Complications**

Hepatitis is common. Non-specific symptoms of fever and malaise may persist for several weeks or occasionally months.

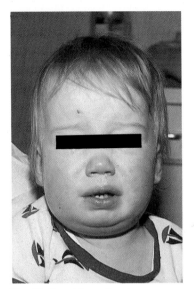

**Fig. 42** Parotid swelling in mumps.

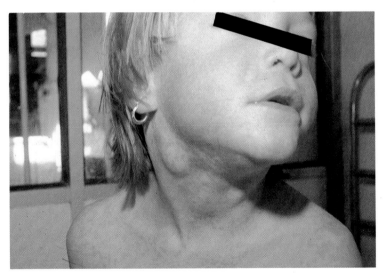

**Fig. 43** Lymphadenopathy and rash in infectious mononucleosis.

# Infection (3)

## Herpes zoster

*Chicken pox (varicella)*

**Clinical features**

Incubation period 14–21 days. The spots occur in crops which rapidly progress from macules to papules to vesicles (Fig. 44). The vesicle becomes crusted and the child remains infectious until the scales separate 10–14 days later, often leaving pitted scars.

**Complications**

Chicken pox is usually a mild illness, except when the child is immunodeficient. Encephalitis is rare, but when it occurs the predominant sign is ataxia with onset several weeks after the acute illness. Haemorrhagic chicken pox (Fig. 45) is a very uncommon, but severe form of the illness.

*Shingles (herpes zoster)*

Uncommon in children. Vesicles have the typical dermatome distribution (Fig. 46). Itching is a common symptom, but post-herpetic neuralgia is rare.

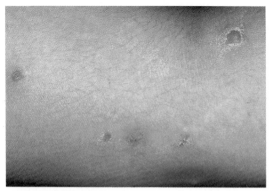

**Fig. 44** Chicken pox.

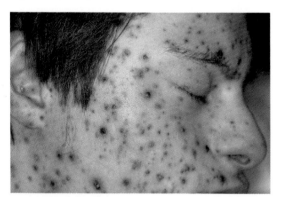

**Fig. 45** Haemorrhagic chicken pox.

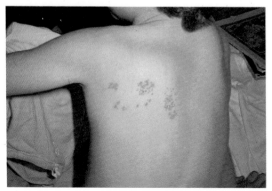

**Fig. 46** Shingles.

# Infection (4)

## Herpes simplex

**Clinical features**

Primary herpes simplex infection may produce a severe gingivostomatitis in young children. Multiple painful blisters or ulcers occur around the mouth, on the lips (Figs 47, 49) and buccal mucous membranes. The child is usually extremely miserable with excessive dribbling and salivation, fever, irritability and difficulty in swallowing. Recurrent herpes simplex causes the simple common cold sore.

**Complications**

Dehydration may occur when there is inadequate fluid intake because of the painful mouth and difficulty in swallowing. Herpes encephalitis is a rare but serious complication with high mortality and morbidity.

**Management**

Sympathetic nursing, analgesia, and adequate fluid intake are necessary. The primary infection is usually self-limiting within 2 weeks. Early infection within 48 hours of onset may respond to topical idoxuridine. Acyclovir is effective for systemic complications.

## Haemophilus cellulitis

**Clinical features**

Haemophilus influenzae occasionally causes severe cellulitis affecting the face, particularly the cheek, periorbital region and neck (Fig. 48).

**Management**

Responds to appropriate antibiotic—usually ampicillin or chloramphenicol.

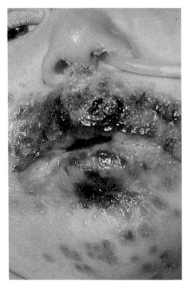

**Fig. 47** Herpes stomatitis.

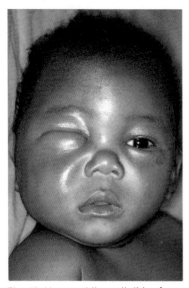

**Fig. 48** Haemophilus cellulitis of the face.

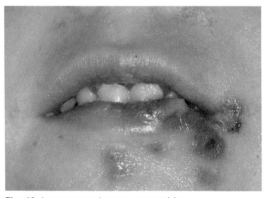

**Fig. 49** Less severe herpes stomatitis.

## Staphylococcal infection

**Clinical features**

Impetigo, the most common superficial staphylococcal infection, is highly contagious. Individual lesions begin as erythematous spots which rapidly increase in size and develop brown crusts (Fig. 50).

Toxic epidermal necrolysis (TEN—scalded skin syndrome) is caused by toxins of staphylococcal phage types 71 or 22. Initially there is intense redness and pain resembling a superficial scald. Minimal trauma may result in a positive Nikolsky's sign (separation of epidermis from dermis because of oedema between the two layers of skin). Generalised exfoliation of the skin often occurs.

**Management**

Systemic antistaphylococcal antibiotic such as flucloxacillin. Tetracycline should never be used in children because of the risk of staining the teeth (Fig. 51). General hygiene such as frequent hand-washing and short clean finger nails will help to limit cross-infection. Nasal carriage of staphylococci in the internal nares will be reduced by the use of antiseptic cream.

## Osteomyelitis

**Clinical features**

90% of cases are caused by *Staphylococcus aureus.* The metaphyses of the long bones are usually affected. There are local signs of acute inflammation and exquisite bony tenderness. Fever and toxaemia often occur.

**Diagnosis and management**

Blood cultures usually identify the organism. Radioisotope bone scan may reveal a 'hot spot' earlier than X-rays, which rarely show any abnormality before the second week. Surgical drainage is sometimes necessary. Systemic antibiotics are given for several months. With adequate treatment, chronic osteomyelitis (Fig. 52) is now rare.

PAEDIATRICS

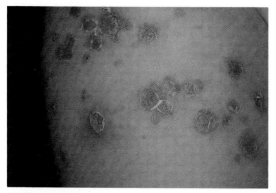

**Fig. 50** Impetigo.

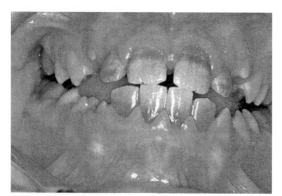

**Fig. 51** Tetracycline staining of teeth.

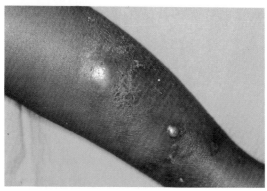

**Fig. 52** Chronic osteomyelitis.

## Meningitis

**Aetiology**

*Haemophilus influenzae*, meningococcal and pneumococcal infection are the most common forms of bacterial meningitis in children under the age of 5 years.

**Clinical features**

Specific signs such as headache and neck stiffness occur in older children but are often absent in young infants. Infants often present with non-specific signs of irritability, drowsiness, vomiting, anorexia, convulsions or fever. Bulging fontanelle, high pitched cry and arching of the back (opisthotonos) (Fig. 53) are late signs.

**Diagnosis**

High index of suspicion in any ill child with unexplained fever or convulsions. Cerebrospinal fluid examination and culture will confirm the diagnosis.

**Management**

Broad spectrum antibiotics until the specific organism and sensitivities are known.

## Meningococcaemia

**Clinical features**

An acute fulminating septicaemia with shock and a purpuric rash (Fig. 54). Meningococcal septicaemia has a high mortality; high dosage intravenous penicillin should be commenced immediately in any ill child with a suspicious rash.

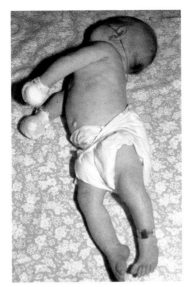

**Fig. 53** Opisthotonos.

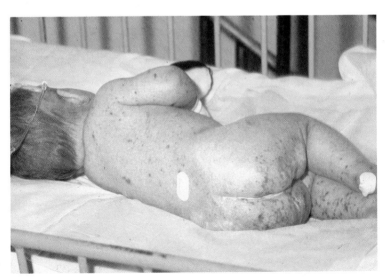

**Fig. 54** Meningococcal septicaemia.

## Erysipelas

**Aetiology**    Streptococcal skin infection.

**Clinical features**    Spreading cellulitis with a well-defined edge (Fig. 55). A red flare is sometimes seen spreading along the lymphatic drainage.

**Management**    High dosage penicillin.

## Tuberculosis

**Aetiology**    *Mycobacterium tuberculosis.* Primary infection may present in the lung or as enlarged lymph nodes. It is contracted by droplet spread, usually from asymptomatic adults.

**Clinical features**    Primary tuberculosis is usually asymptomatic. Haematogenous spread and meningitis are most common in the very young, and in children with malnutrition or intercurrent infection. Pulmonary tuberculosis with chronic cough occurs in later life.

**Diagnosis**    Sensitivity to tuberculin as shown by a positive Mantoux reaction (Fig. 55) develops within 4−8 weeks after infection. CXR may show hilar lymphadenopathy or a segmental lesion.

**Managment**    Combination chemotherapy with isoniazid, rifampicin, and sometimes ethambutol, ethionamide or PAS for at least 12 months.

**Prevention**    BCG vaccination gives up to 80% protection again tuberculosis.

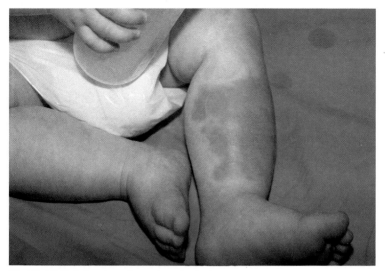

**Fig. 55** Well-defined erythema (erysipelas).

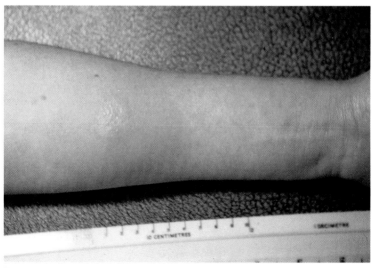

**Fig. 56** Positive Mantoux reaction.

# 5 | Skin Disorders (1)

## Eczema

**Incidence**

Common; affects 3% of children. Onset usually within first 2 years of life.

**Inheritance**

Often family history of other atopic disorders, e.g. asthma, hay-fever, allergy.

**Clinical features**

Itchy plaques with excoriation and lichenification (Fig. 57), characteristically occurring on the face, behind the knees, antecubital fossae and wrists, but can occur anywhere (Fig. 58). The skin is often dry and itching is a prominent symptom. Secondary infection is common because of scratching.

**Investigation**

Eosinophilia, raised serum IgE or positive skin tests are sometimes helpful in the general diagnosis of atopy, but rarely useful in clinical management, as multiple factors are usually involved.

**Management**

Soap should be avoided and emollient oil or emulsifying ointment used instead. Aqueous cream can be used liberally on the dry skin. Weak corticosteroid cream may be applied sparingly to bad patches during acute flare-ups. Systemic antihistamines are somtimes useful to control itching and scratching, which occur particularly during sleep. When there is a clear history of aggravation by certain foods, an exclusion diet may help.

**Course and prognosis**

Fluctuating course, usually with improvement in later childhood.

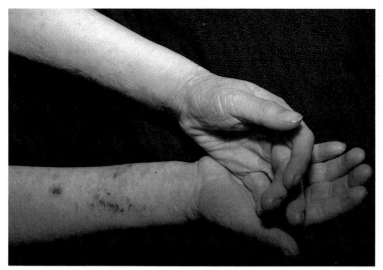

**Fig. 57** Typical eczematous rash on arms.

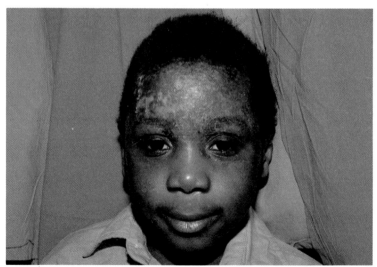

**Fig. 58** Eczema on face.

## 5 | Skin Disorders (2)

### Napkin or diaper rash

**Aetiology**

Usually due to irritation from prolonged wearing of wet napkins—sometimes called 'ammonical dermatitis'. Monilial infection and seborrhoeic dermatitis are the other main rashes in the napkin area.

**Clinical features**

Erythema, umbilicated pustules, and ulceration of the perineum and sometimes the genitalia (Fig. 59), but usually sparing the groin flexures. The presence of discrete satellite lesions or involvement of the flexures is suggestive of monilial infection (Fig. 60). In babies with loose stools, there is often perianal eythema.

**Management**

Napkins should be changed frequently. In simple napkin rash, exposure of the perineum and a protective barrier cream is all that is required. Monilial infection responds to topical nystatin or miconazole cream. *Monilia* should always be considered when a rash does not respond to simple treatment. Seborrhoeic dermatitis often requires the application of a weak steroid cream.

PAEDIATRICS

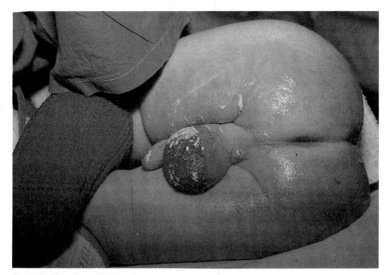

**Fig. 59** Simple napkin rash.

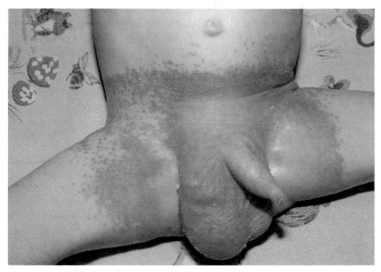

**Fig. 60** Monilial infection with discrete satellite lesions.

## 5 | Skin Disorders (3)

## Seborrhoeic dermatitis

Very common in young infants; aetiology unknown.

**Clinical features**

Distinctive greasy, scaly, erythematous rash or plaques (Fig. 61), which usually appear within the first few months of life. The eyebrows, skin behind the ears, and perineum are commonly affected. Thick greasy scales are often found on the scalp where the condition is commonly called 'cradle cap' (Fig. 63). Occasionally there may be discoid lesions on the trunk spreading up from a napkin rash (napkin psoriasis) (Fig. 62). In mild forms, seborrhoeic dermatitis may be mistakenly diagnosed as atopic eczema, particularly when the rash affects the flexures. There is never any systemic illness, even with widespread seborrhoeic dermatitis (Leiner's syndrome), but secondary infection sometimes occurs.

**Management**

Mild corticosteroid cream such as 1% hydrocortisone. Cradle cap usually responds to a keratolytic shampoo or cream, but often recurs.

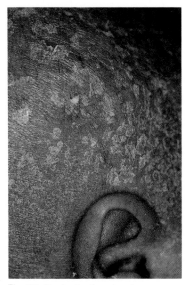

**Fig. 61** Typical seborrhoeic plaques.

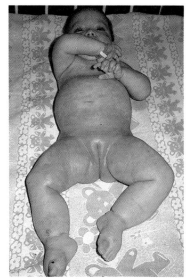

**Fig. 62** Napkin psoriasis.

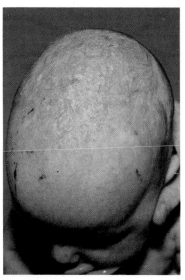

**Fig. 63** Cradle cap

| # Skin Disorders (4)

## Urticaria

**Aetiology**

A common allergic manifestation, but the offending allergen is often not identified. Some recurrent cases are caused by sensitivity to food colouring agents.

**Clinical features**

Intensely itchy, erythematous rash with wheals. The pattern of the rash is constantly changing and may leave areas of bruising when the wheals subside (Fig. 64). There is often marked oedema, particularly around the eyes and mouth, where it is called 'angioneurotic oedema' (Fig. 66).

**Management**

Acute respiratory obstruction caused by severe swelling of the mouth and tongue may be life-threatening; it responds to subcutaneous adrenaline. Systemic antihistamines may be helpful in urticaria. Food exclusion diets may help some children with recurrent urticaria. Some cases of chronic or recurrent urticaria are due to familial acetyl-cholinesterase deficiency.

## Stevens-Johnson syndrome

**Aetiology**

A rare, idiosyncratic reaction usually to drugs such as penicillin or sulphonamides.

**Clinical features**

Begins as a bullous eruption which rapidly progresses to widespread skin loss (Fig. 65). There is always involvement of the mucous membranes of the mouth, rectum, vagina or conjunctiva.

**Management**

Discontinue the offending drug. Barrier nursing, strict fluid and electrolyte balance and prevention of infection are important. In severe cases, mortality is high, particularly if septicaemia occurs.

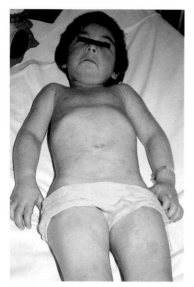

**Fig. 64** Urticaria.

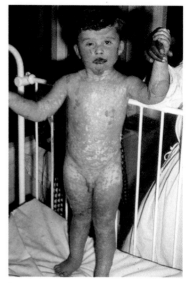

**Fig. 65** Stevens-Johnson syndrome.

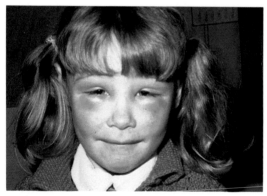

**Fig. 66** Angioneurotic oedema.

## 5 | Skin Disorders (5)

### Henoch-Schönlein purpura

| | |
|---|---|
| **Synonym** | Anaphylactoid purpura. |
| **Incidence** | Common; often occurs in small epidemics. |
| **Aetiology** | Diffuse vasculitis of unknown aetiology; there is often a history of a recent viral upper respiratory tract infection. |
| **Clinical features** | The pathognomonic feature is a purpuric rash on the buttocks, extensor surfaces of the legs, and arms (Figs. 67–69), and sometimes the face. The lesions are often papular and bullae are sometimes present. Localised oedema of the face, hands, feet and scrotum often accompany the typical rash, and flitting arthritis affecting the large peripheral joints is common. Colicky abdominal pain is a troublesome symptom and haematemesis, melaena or intussusception occur in a minority of cases. Haematuria occurs in approximately 70% of children with Henoch-Schönlein purpura, but progressive renal disease occurs in less than 1%. |
| **Management** | Other causes of purpura should always be excluded. Treatment is symptomatic; and analgesia and bed-rest are usually all that is required. Corticosteroids may be indicated if there are severe gastrointestinal symptoms or progressive renal involvement. |
| **Course and prognosis** | The majority resolve rapidly, although further episodes or recurrences are common in the first few weeks. The prognosis is more serious if acute nephritis or nephrotic syndrome is present. |

PAEDIATRICS

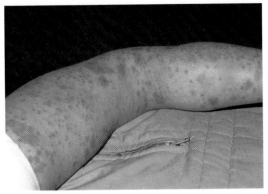

**Fig. 67** Typical purpura on the leg.

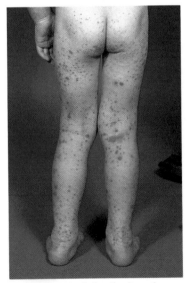

**Fig. 68** Classical distribution of Henoch-Schönlein purpura.

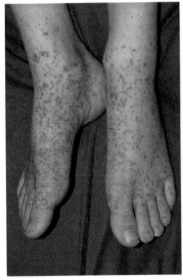

**Fig. 69** Purpura on feet.

## Erythema nodosum

**Incidence**
Common, particularly in black children.

**Aetiology**
May be associated with streptococcal infection, tuberculosis, sarcoidosis, *Mycoplasma* infection, drug sensitivity (particularly to sulphonamides), or inflammatory bowel disease. In the majority of cases, no underlying condition will be found.

**Clinical features**
Exquisitely tender, raised erythematous nodules most frequently occurring over the pretibial region (Fig. 70), but may also occur around the elbows and on the forearms. They often occur in crops over a period of several weeks or occasionally months, and may be associated with fever and arthralgia, particularly when the nodules occur over joints. The skin lesions resolve into the same colour changes as a bruise.

## Dermoid cysts

**Aetiology**
Development anomalies that are found along the suture lines of the skull.

**Clinical features**
Firm, non-tender subcutaneous swellings typically found around the orbit or in the midline of the skull anywhere from the occiput to the base of the nose. The most common site is at the lateral margin of the orbit where the dermoid cyst is known as an 'external angular dermoid' (Fig. 71).

**Course and prognosis**
Dermoid cysts usually increase slowly in size. They sometimes become infected.

**Management**
Surgery to remove the dermoid cyst is usually required for cosmetic reasons or because of recurrent infection.

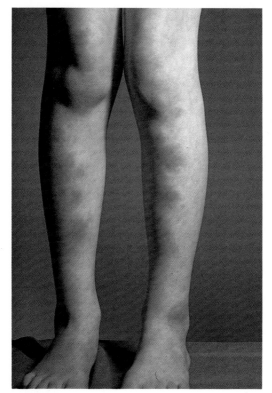

**Fig. 70** Erythema nodosum.

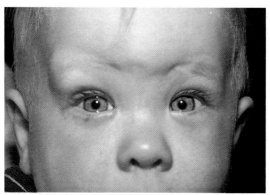

**Fig. 71** External angular dermoid.

## 5 | Skin Disorders (7)

### Fungal infections and infestations

*Scabies*
Intensely itchy, excoriated, erythematous papular rash (Fig. 72), sometimes with burrows visible to the naked eye. Scabies may occur anywhere on the body, but is said to be most common between the fingers and around the wrists. Scabies is spread by close human contact. The whole family should be treated with topical gamma benzene hexachloride; clothes and bed-linen should be thoroughly washed if recurrence is to be avoided.

*Tinea*
Tinea (ringworm) causes circular erythematous patches with a scaly centre. When tinea affects the scalp, there may be hair loss with circular patches of baldness. Tinea corporis usually responds to topical antifungals such as miconazole. Systemic griseofulvin may be necessary when there is extensive hair or nail involvement.

*Monilia*
Oral thrush is common in young infants. *Candida* also gives rise to a characteristic napkin rash with erythematous ulcerated satellite lesions. In later childhood, oral thrush may occur when the child is taking corticosteroids or when there is an immunodeficiency syndrome (Fig. 73).

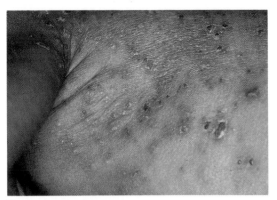

**Fig. 72** Scabies infestation with excoriation.

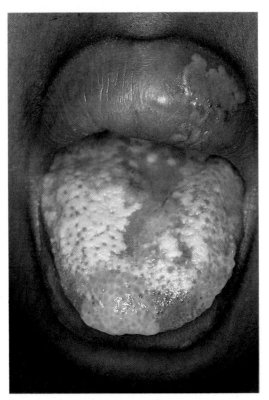

**Fig. 73** Oral thrush with severe ulceration.

## 5 | Skin Disorders (8)

### Psoriasis

**Incidence**

Uncommon in childhood, and when it occurs there is usually a strong family history.

**Aetiology**

Unknown.

**Clinical features**

Erythematous, scaly lesions which form plaques (Figs 74, 75) typically on the elbows, knees, around the hairline and scalp. When the lesion is scratched lightly, it produces a pearly appearance.

**Management and course**

The tendency to psoriasis is usually life-long. Treatment depends on the severity of the lesions. Corticosteroids, coal-tar and salicylic acid ointments are the mainstay of treatment.

### Cavernous haemangioma

**Incidence and aetiology**

Common congenital malformation of blood vessels usually involving skin or mucous membrane.

**Clinical features**

Often large blood-filled channels located deeply in the subcutaneous or submucous areas (Fig. 76).

**Management**

Treatment may be required if there is significant bleeding, thrombocytopenia or cosmetic embarrassment. Surgical excision is often difficult; sclerosing agents are sometimes used.

**Fig. 74** Severe psoriasis.

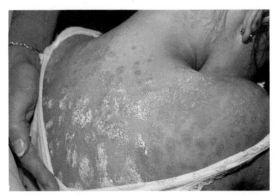

**Fig. 75** Multiple plaques of psoriasis.

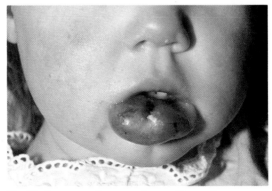

**Fig. 76** Cavernous haemangioma of lower lip.

## Kawasaki's disease

**Synonyms** | Mucocutaneous lymph node syndrome (MLNS).

**Incidence** | Most common in Japan, but reported worldwide.

**Clinical features** | Prolonged febrile illness with fleeting erythematous rash, sore tongue, cracked lips and lymphadenopathy. During the second week after the fever has subsided, there is typical peeling of the hands and feet (Fig. 77).

**Mangement** | Cardiac complications associated with thrombocytosis occur in a minority of children. Salicylates and dipyridamole may prevent the development of coronary artery aneurysms.

## Keloid

**Clinical features** | Excessive scar formation (Fig. 78) often after minimal trauma. Common in negroid population.

**Management** | Surgical excision is difficult because of the tendency to increasing keloid formation.

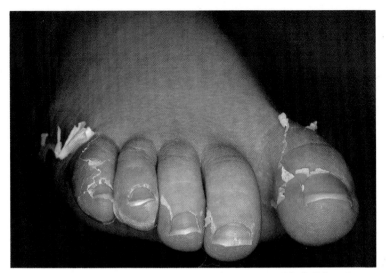

**Fig. 77** Peeling toes in Kawasaki's disease. (By courtesy of Dr R. Briggs.)

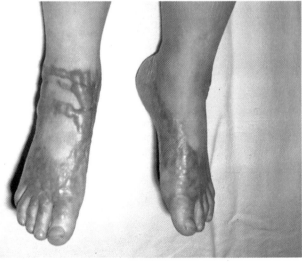

**Fig. 78** Keloid after burns.

## Alopecia areata

**Incidence**

Uncommon; alopecia areata totalis is very rare. There is an increased incidence in Down's syndrome.

**Aetiology**

Unknown; but sometimes occurs during periods of stress.

**Clinical features**

Alopecia areata commonly causes localised hair loss on the scalp. It can usually be distinguished from tinea capitis by the characteristic margin of exclamation mark hair shafts, and the absence of erythema and scaling (Fig. 79).

**Course and prognosis**

Usually self-limiting; but occasionally may progress to alopecia totalis, which results in total body hair loss. There is no effective treatment.

## Pigmented naevi

**Clinical features**

Discrete brown or black pigmented skin lesions. The lesion is usually not elevated during childhood, but may become palpable during adult life. Some congenital pigmented naevi contain hair follicles (Fig. 80). Multiple pigmented naevi are seen in certain syndromes such as neurofibromatosis.

**Management**

Junctional naevi occasionally develop into malignant melanoma in adults, but this is rare. The majority of pigmented naevi are harmless (Fig. 81). Surgical excision, or dermabrasion may be required for cosmetic reasons.

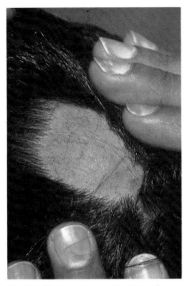

**Fig. 79** Scalp hair loss in alopecia areata.

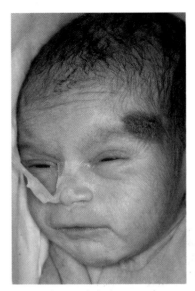

**Fig. 80** Congenital pigmented hairy naevus.

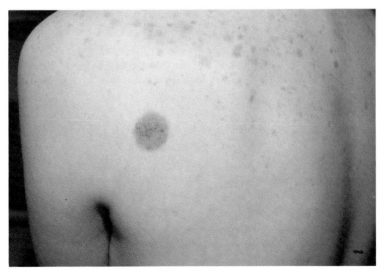

**Fig. 81** Multiple pigmented naevi.

| # Gastrointestinal Disorders (1)

## Gastroenteritis

**Incidence**

Commonest cause of death in young infants in developing countries where early weaning and malnutrition are common.

**Aetiology**

Rotavirus infection is a common cause of gastroenteritis in infants in winter months. *E. coli, Salmonella, Shigella* and *Campylobacter* are the common causes of bacterial gastroenteritis.

**Clinical features**

Diarrhoea, vomiting and colicky abdominal pain. The most serious complication is dehydration due to excessive water loss or inadequate fluid intake. In mild to moderate dehydration (up to 5%) the child is thirsty, lethargic, has sunken eyes and loss of skin turgor (Figs 82,83). In moderate to severe dehydration (5–10%) there may be tachycardia and signs of peripheral circulatory collapse.

**Management**

Recognition of dehydration and adequate fluid and electrolyte replacement is important. Frequent administration of an oral glucose electrolyte solution is usually possible, except when there is shock. Intravenous therapy will then be necessary.

## Intestinal parasites

**Incidence**

Common cause of malabsorption, anaemia and chronic diarrhoea in developing countries.

**Aetiology and clinical features**

*Giardia lamblia* is a protozoal infestation which causes acute diarrhoea and sometimes chronic malabsorption. *Ascaris lumbricoides* (roundworm) (Fig. 84) causes colicky abdominal pain and gut obstruction. *Ankylostoma* (hookworm) is a common cause of iron deficiency anaemia in tropical countries.

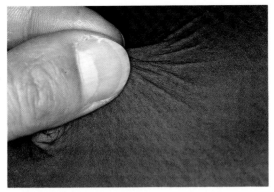

**Fig. 82** Dehydration with dry skin.

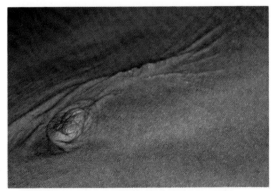

**Fig. 83** Dehydration showing poor skin turgor after release.

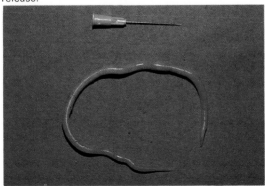

**Fig. 84** *Ascaris lumbricoides* (roundworm).

| **Gastrointestinal Disorders (2)**

## Coeliac disease

**Synonyms**

Gluten sensitivity; gluten intolerance.

**Aetiology**

Permanent intolerance of dietary wheat, rye and sometimes barley and oats.

**Incidence**

About 1 in 2000 in the UK; recent impression is that coeliac disease is becoming less common.

**Clinical features**

Most children have signs within the first 2 years of life. There may be poor weight gain after introduction of gluten-containing solids, but signs are often more insidious. Vomiting, diarrhoea and abdominal distension are common. Anorexia, irritability with miserable facies (Fig. 85), hypotonia and wasted buttocks (Figs 86, 87) occur. Sometimes failure to thrive or growth failure is the only sign.

**Diagnosis**

Jejunal biopsy, showing total villous atrophy and inflammatory infiltration of the lamina propria, is the definitive investigation.

**Management**

Gluten-free diet. Supplementation with iron and vitamins is often necessary after diagnosis. Lactose or cow's milk protein intolerance sometimes occur.

**Course and prognosis**

Gastrointestinal symptoms, mood disturbance and growth failure improve with a gluten-free diet. There is an increased risk of intestinal lymphoma in adult life.

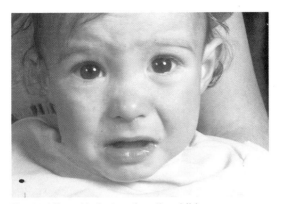

**Fig. 85** Miserable facies of coeliac child.

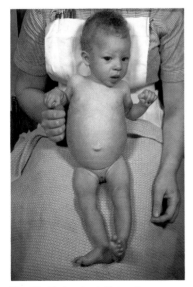

**Fig. 86** Abdominal distension.

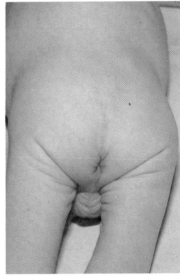

**Fig. 87** Abdominal distension and wasted buttocks.

# 6 | Gastrointestinal Disorders (3)

## Pyloric stenosis

**Aetiology**

Hypertrophy of the smooth muscle of pylorus of obscure aetiology. First born male infants often affected. Possible recent increase in incidence.

**Clinical features**

Onset of vomiting within a few weeks of birth; classically, projectile vomiting with failure to thrive and constipation. During feeding, a pyloric mass can usually be palpated and visible peristalsis may be seen in the upper abdomen (Fig. 88)

**Management**

Surgery (Ramstedt's pyloromyotomy) after rehydration and correction of electrolyte imbalance.

## Intussusception

**Incidence**

Common cause of gut obstruction in infancy.

**Clinical features**

Sudden onset of colicky abdominal pain, with loose stools often blood-stained (red-currant jelly stools). A sausage-shaped bowel mass may be palpable.

**Management**

Gentle barium enema (Fig. 89) will confirm the diagnosis and may be curative in cases of recent onset. Surgery may be required for intus-susception when the diagnosis is delayed.

## Hirschsprung's disease

**Aetiology**

Absence of ganglionic cells in the colon.

**Clinical features**

May cause acute neonatal intestinal obstruction (Fig. 90), or chronic constipation in older children.

**Management**

Barium enema, and anorectal manometry assist in the diagnosis; rectal biopsy is always necessary for confirmation. Colostomy relieves the acute obstruction; resection of the aganglionic segment and a pull-through anastomosis are performed later.

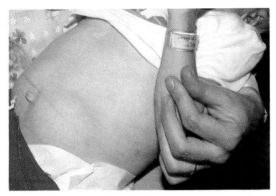

**Fig. 88** Visible peristalsis in pyloric stenosis.

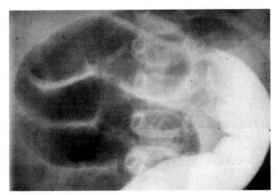

**Fig. 89** Intussusception.

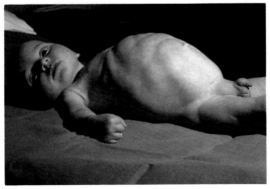

**Fig. 90** Distended abdomen in Hirschsprung's disease. (By courtesy of Dr T. Lissauer.)

# 7 | **Genitourinary Disorders (1)**

## Hypospadias

Commonest minor abnormality of the male genitalia; occurs in 1 in 350 boys. Malposition of the urethral orifice varies in severity from perineal (Fig. 91) to glandular. Ventral curvature (chordee; Fig. 92) may occur on erection and is an indication for surgery. Circumcision should not be performed until reconstructive plastic surgery has been considered.

## Circumcision

The prepuce is closely adherent to the glans during early childhood and retraction is unnecessary and undesirable. Spontaneous separation occurs after some years. The only medical indications for circumcision are phimosis, paraphimosis, and recurrent balanitis.

## Undescended testes

Undescended testes are common in young infants; exploration and orchidopexy is indicated if the testes fail to descend by 1 year of age. Retractile testes due to an active cremasteric reflex are extremely common and entirely normal.

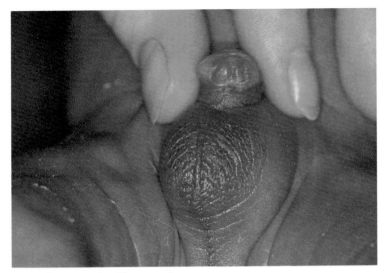

**Fig. 91** Severe perineal hypospadias.

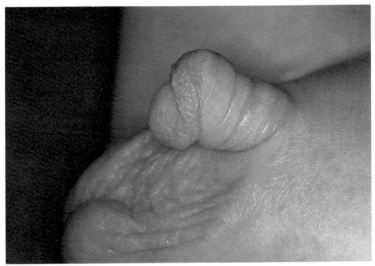

**Fig. 92** Ventral curvature of penis (chordee).

## Nephrotic syndrome

**Incidence**

1 in 20 000 children; boys more commonly affected; peak age incidence 1–5 years.

**Aetiology**

Cause unknown; immunological basis likely.

**Clinical features**

Periorbital (Fig. 93) and generalised oedema, abdominal pain, ascites. Gross proteinuria may lead to hypovolaemia and acute circulatory collapse. Prone to pneumococcal peritonitis.

**Management**

Bed-rest and high protein, salt restricted diet until diuresis occurs, usually within 10–14 days of starting oral corticosteroids. Hypovolaemia responds to infusion of plasma or salt-free albumin.

**Course and prognosis**

Majority have minimal change lesion and recover completely within 2 years. Relapses are common, but normally respond to steroids. Cyclophosphamide therapy occasionally necessary.

## Inguinal herniae and hydroceles

Both are due to persistent patency of the processus vaginalis. Hydroceles in the newborn usually resolve spontaneously within the first year, but in older boys, surgery will be necessary. Inguinal herniae (Fig. 94) always require surgery, and the risk of strangulation is high, particularly in young infants.

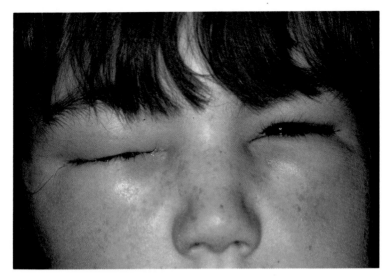

**Fig. 93** Periorbital oedema in nephrotic syndrome.

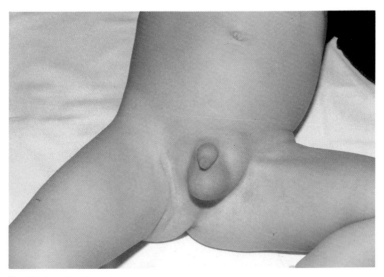

**Fig. 94** Inguinal hernia.

## 7 | Genitourinary disorders (3)

### Urinary tract infection (UTI)

**Incidence**

Very common infection; occurs in 1–2% of girls.

**Clinical features**

The young child usually has non-specific symptoms of poor weight gain, fever, vomiting and irritability. Older children may complain of urinary frequency, dysuria and loin pain.

**Diagnosis**

High index of suspicion; must obtain adequate urine sample for urinalysis and culture. Suprapubic aspirate is often necessary in young infants because skin contamination may make bag or clean-catch specimens difficult to interpret, particularly in girls.

**Management**

Acute infection requires antibiotic therapy. All proven UTIs require investigation of the renal tract with ultrasound examination, intravenous urogram, and sometimes radioisotope scans or micturating cystourethrogram. At least 50% have an underlying abnormality, most commonly vesicoureteric reflux (Fig. 95). Prophylactic antibiotics may protect against renal scarring during growth. Surgery is occasionally necessary and usually involves ureteric reimplantation.

### Renal tract anomalies

**Incidence**

Relatively common; most are asymptomatic and functionally insignificant.

**Clinical features**

Ureteric duplication is usually asymptomatic but may predispose to infection, obstruction or reflux. Posterior urethral valves in male infants cause poor urinary stream, and obstruction may cause renal failure. Horseshoe kidneys, pelvic kidneys, unilateral renal dysplasia are often asymptomatic unless there is infection. Severe anomalies of the renal tract such as renal agenesis or prune-belly syndrome (Fig. 96) are usually diagnosed shortly after birth.

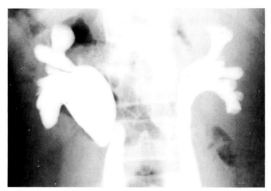

**Fig. 95** Vesicoureteric reflux (bilateral grade III).

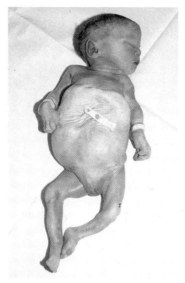

**Fig. 96** Prune-belly syndrome.

# Cardiorespiratory Disorders (1)

## Congenital heart disease

**Incidence**

Common; at least 1 in 300 live births.

**Aetiology**

Usually unknown; sometimes associated with chromosomal abnormality or rubella embryopathy.

**Clinical features**

Asymptomatic cardiac murmurs are often heard during routine examination. Cyanosis (Fig. 97) or heart failure usually indicate a serious structural defect. Clubbing of the fingers and toes (Fig. 98) may develop in conditions such as Fallot's tetralogy when there is long-standing cyanosis.

**Investigation**

CXR and ECG are often helpful, but rarely diagnostic. Ultrasound examination and cardiac catheterisation give more precise detail of cardiac structure. When coarctation of the aorta is suspected because of inequality or delay of femoral pulses, blood pressure must be measured and a difference between the upper and lower limbs is significant.

**Management**

Depends on underlying problem. The most common abnormality is a ventricular septal defect (VSD). The majority of VSDs close spontaneously or become functionally insignificant in later childhood. Surgery is usually required for more serious defects.

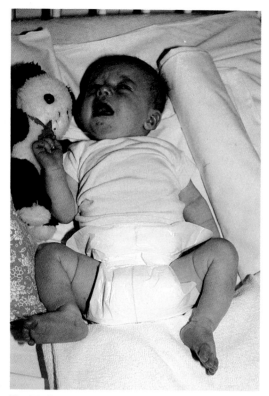

**Fig. 97** Cyanotic congenital heart disease.

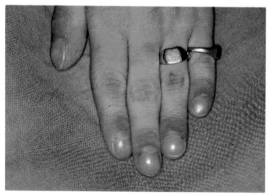

**Fig. 98** Finger clubbing in cyanotic heart disease.

## Bronchiolitis

**Incidence**
Commonly occurs in infants in winter epidemics; usually due to respiratory syncytial virus (RSV).

**Clinical features**
Coryzal symptoms, then gradual onset of cough, wheeze, tachypnoea and feeding difficulty. May develop over-inflation of the lungs, producing a barrel-shaped chest, cyanosis, subcostal recession (Fig. 99) and occasionally heart failure.

**Management**
Supportive care with added oxygen when necessary. Tube feeding or intravenous fluids are often required. Antibiotics are not usually indicated, but may be given if secondary infection is suspected or in a very ill child. Treatment of cardiac failure or mechanical ventilation is occasionally necessary.

## Asthma

**Incidence**
A very common respiratory illness in childhood; 1 in 7 children affected.

**Aetiology**
Allergens, particularly house dust mite, always important in children. There is often a family history of asthma, allergies or eczema.

**Clinical features**
Mild asthmatics may have only chronic cough, particularly nocturnal or exercise-induced. More severe symptoms include wheezing, and respiratory distress. Children with chronic under-treated asthma may develop chest deformity (Fig. 100) and growth failure.

**Management**
Severity of attack best assessed by monitoring peak flow. Acute bronchospasm usually responds to inhaled beta-sympathomimetics or xanthines. Prophylaxis with inhaled sodium cromoglycate or corticosteroids is helpful in chronic asthma.

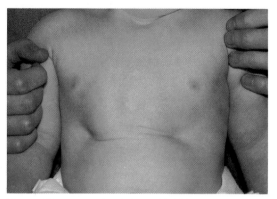

**Fig. 99** Chest recession in bronchiolitis.

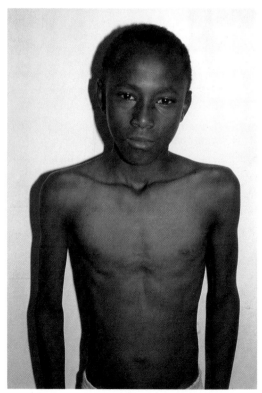

**Fig. 100** Chest deformity in a chronic asthmatic.

# Cardiorespiratory Disorders (3)

## Acute laryngotracheobronchitis
### (croup)

| | |
|---|---|
| **Incidence** | Common in young children under 4 years of age; usually viral illness. |
| **Clinical features** | Coryzal symptoms for several days, then development of a characteristic barking cough and inspiratory stridor (croup). Symptoms often worse at night or when child is anxious or crying. When cyanosis or subcostal recession are present, the child should be observed in hospital. |
| **Management** | There is no evidence that humidification, steroids or antibiotics are of any value, but they are sometimes used. Oxygen should be provided when there are signs of hypoxia. Occasionally tracheal intubation may be required if there is severe airways obstruction or exhaustion. |

## Acute epiglottitis

| | |
|---|---|
| **Incidence** | Uncommon, but potentially fatal. Occurs in children aged 4–10 years. |
| **Aetiology** | *Haemophilus influenzae* type B infection of epiglottis. |
| **Clinical features** | Sudden onset of severe stridor and upper airways obstruction. Children rapidly become toxic and develop life-threatening obstruction within a few hours. |
| **Management** | Examination of the epiglottis should only be attempted when there is immediate expert provision for maintaining an adequate airway. Tracheal intubation (Fig. 101) is often necessary, but frequently difficult. Tracheostomy (Fig. 102) is occasionally unavoidable. |
| | Intravenous ampicillin and chloramphenicol usually control the oedema and inflammation of the epiglottis within a few days. |

PAEDIATRICS

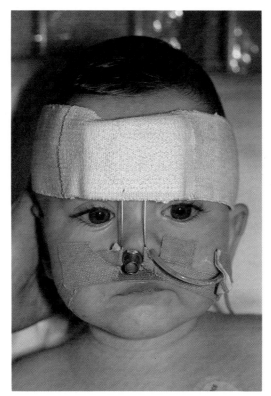

**Fig. 101** Nasal intubation for acute epiglottitis.

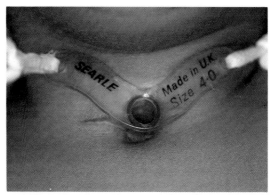

**Fig. 102** Tracheostomy.

# Cardiorespiratory Disorders (4)

## Pneumonia

**Aetiology**

In infancy, bronchopneumonia is usually caused by *Haemophilus influenzae* or rarely by *Staphylococcus aureus*. Pneumococcal infection may cause lobar pneumonia in older children.

**Clinical features**

Fever, tachypnoea, meningism and feeding difficulties are common. Localising signs are often absent in young infants, so CXR is usually necessary in any ill child (Fig. 103). Recurrent chest infections or localised air-trapping is sometimes due to inhalation of a foreign body.

**Management**

Broad spectrum antibiotics until specific organism and sensitivities identified.

## Cystic fibrosis

**Incidence**

Commonest cause of suppurative chronic lung disease and pancreatic insufficiency in children in UK, USA and Australia. Autosomal recessive inheritance; carrier rate in general population is 1 in 20. Cystic fibrosis affects 1 in 1600 live births.

**Aetiology**

Abnormality of exocrine and mucus-secreting glands; aetiology unknown. Carriers are asymptomatic and undetectable by current methods.

**Clinical features**

Affected neonates may have meconium ileus and gut obstruction. Usually have recurrent chest infections (Fig. 104), failure to thrive and malabsorption within the first few years of life. Diagnosis confirmed by sweat test.

**Management**

Pancreatic extract supplements control the pancreatic insufficiency and malabsorption. Prompt and aggressive treatment of chest infections with antibiotics and postural drainage. Prophylactic antibiotics may be helpful. Long-term survival into adult life depends on severity of chest involvement. Chronic chest deformity and infections caused by antibiotic-resistant organisms frequently develop.

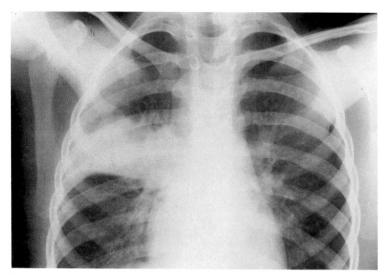

**Fig. 103** Lobar pneumonia.

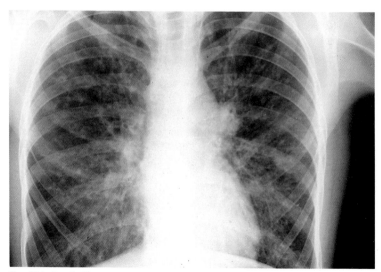

**Fig. 104** Cystic fibrosis.

## 9 | Neuromuscular and Joint Disorders (1)

### Meningomyelocele (spina bifida)

**Management and complications**

After neonatal surgery, a variety of specialist help will be required. Surgical closure of the spinal defect (Fig. 105) is usually not difficult, but long-term complications are common. Urinary incontinence and urinary tract infections are common and distressing. Congenital dislocation of the hips and talipes equinovarus are frequent orthopaedic complications. Hydrocephalus often requires insertion of a shunt.

**Prognosis**

Despite the long-term complications, with sympathetic and careful early assessment, many children lead rewarding and meaningful lives.

### Hydrocephalus

**Aetiology**

Congenital aqueduct stenosis; or secondary to meningitis or haemorrhage.

**Clinical features**

Rapid growth of cerebral ventricles and head circumference. Setting-sun eyes (Fig. 106), crack-pot percussion sign and positive transillumination are late signs of hydrocephalus

**Management**

Once the diagnosis is confirmed by serial measurements, ultrasound or CT scan, shunt surgery is usually necessary (Fig. 107).

**Prognosis**

With early diagnosis, prognosis is good for uncomplicated hydrocephalus, but depends on the underlying cause.

PAEDIATRICS

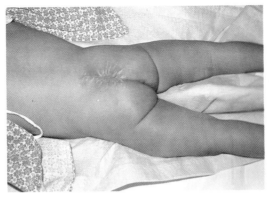

**Fig. 105** Repaired meningomyelocele.

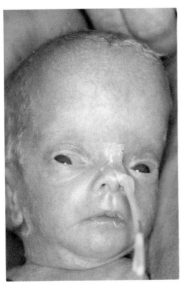

**Fig. 106** Setting-sun eye sign.

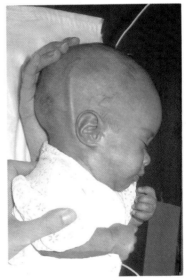

**Fig. 107** Ventriculoperitoneal shunt.

## 9 | Neuromuscular and Joint Disorders (2)

### Cerebral palsy

**Incidence**

2 per 1000 live births.

**Aetiology**

Precise cause is often obscure—some cases are due to anoxic brain damage in fetal or early neonatal life. More common in small, preterm babies.

**Clinical features**

Permanent, but non-progressive disorder of movement and posture. Clinical features often change because child is continuing to grow and develop. Infants often show poor sucking, feeding difficulties, hypotonia, hypertonia, or irritability. Cerebral palsy is often not diagnosed for several months, when delayed or abnormal motor development become more obvious. 70% children with cerebral palsy have spastic manifestations with scissoring of legs (Fig. 108), opisthotonus, hypertonia, clonus and brisk tendon reflexes. One or several limbs may be involved, giving rise to hemiplegia, diplegia or quadriplegia. Ataxic cerebral palsy with hypotonia and weakness occurs in approximately 10%. Choreoathetosis characterised by irregular involuntary movements accounts for another 10% and is sometimes associated with hyperbilirubinaemia (kernicterus).

**Complications**

Mental retardation, epilepsy and sensory handicap are present in at least 60% of children with cerebral palsy.

**Management**

A multidisciplinary approach to assessment and long-term management is essential. Physiotherapy may encourage normal motor development and prevent contractures. The 'wind-swept' deformity (Fig. 109) seen after prolonged immobilisation should be avoidable.

PAEDIATRICS

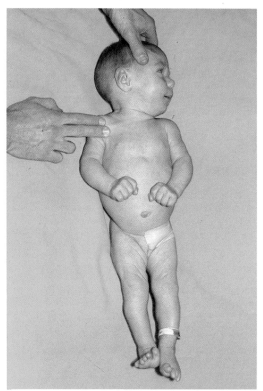

**Fig. 108** Scissoring of legs.

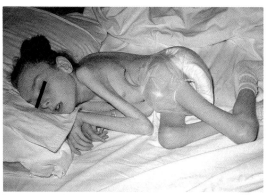

**Fig. 109** 'Wind-swept' deformity.

## 9 | Neuromuscular and Joint Disorders (3)

### Duchenne muscular dystrophy

**Incidence**

Commonest muscular dystrophy; occurs in 1 in 4000 male infants.

**Inheritance**

Sex-linked recessive, but mutations are frequent. Female carriers are often asymptomatic but can often be identified.

**Clinical features**

Usually presents within the first 5 years because of difficulty in climbing stairs and frequent falls. The calf muscles are prominent (Fig. 110) though weak. When attempting to rise to standing from sitting or lying position, the boy 'climbs up' his legs using his hands for support (Gower's sign).

**Diagnosis**

Elevated CPK; abnormal EMG and muscle biopsy.

**Course and prognosis**

Progressive weakness resulting in most boys being confined to a wheelchair by teenage years. Death, usually from respiratory infections, occurs in early adult life.

**Antenatal diagnosis**

Affected male fetus can be identified.

### Werdnig-Hoffmann disease
#### (spinal muscular atrophy)

Occurs in 1 in 20 000 live births.
Autosomal recessive inheritance.
Infants often weak and floppy from birth (Fig. 111).
Rapidly progressive with death from respiratory failure within 12–18 months.

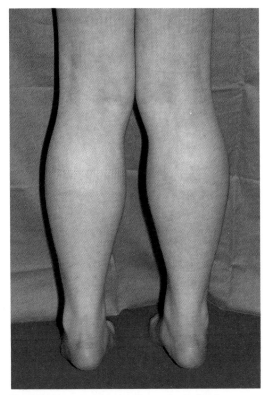

**Fig. 110** Hypertrophied calf muscles in Duchenne muscular dystrophy

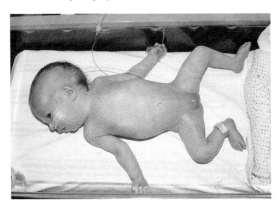

**Fig. 111** Frog-like posture of infant with Werdnig-Hoffmann disease.

# Neuromuscular and Joint Disorders (4)

## The floppy baby

**Aetiology**

Describes clinical condition of hypotonic infant in first year of life. Many underlying causes. Paralytic causes include neuromuscular disorders and cerebral palsy. Non-paralytic causes are hypothyroidism, malnutrition, Down's syndrome. A few floppy infants have delayed, but eventually normal motor development (benign congenital hypotonia). Benign hypotonia is often familial.

**Clinical features**

A useful method of assessment is to hold the young infant in ventral suspension and pull the infant from supine to sitting posture (Fig. 112).

## Arthrogryposis multiplex congenita

**Clinical features**

Clinical syndrome in which there are flexion contractures of muscles and joints, gross muscle wasting and sometimes dislocation of joints (Fig. 113).

**Aetiology**

Usually unknown, may have primary muscle hypoplasia. Sometimes secondary to constricted intrauterine position because of oligohydramnios or uterine abnormality.

**Management**

Long-term physiotherapy may improve contractures. Surgery often helpful later. Long-term prognosis depends on severity of muscular hypoplasia.

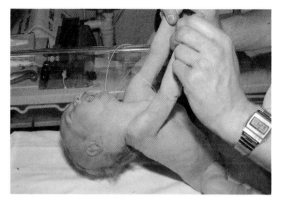

**Fig. 112** Marked head lag of floppy newborn infant.

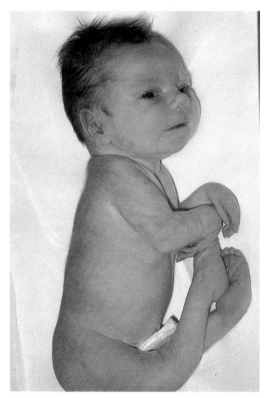

**Fig. 113** Arthrogryposis multiplex congenita.

# Neuromuscular and Joint Disorders (5)

## Poliomyelitis

**Incidence**

Uncommon in countries with successful immunisation policy.

**Clinical features**

Initially a mild viral illness with fever, sore throat, headache and vomiting, lasting several days. About 1 week later, in approximately 30%, there are more severe symptoms of headache, neck stiffness, leg and back pains, and progressive asymmetrical weakness with muscular paralysis due to anterior horn cell damage.

**Course and prognosis**

In severe cases death may occur from respiratory failure and bulbar paralysis in the acute illness. In the majority there is gradual improvement over 12–18 months. Many children have residual muscle wasting and paralysis (Fig. 114).

## Neurofibromatosis

**Synonym**

Von Recklinghausen's disease.

**Incidence**

1 in 3000 live births.

**Inheritance**

Autosomal dominant; but at least 50% due to new mutation.

**Clinical features**

Most have areas of skin hypo- or hyperpigmentation (café-au-lait spots) (Fig. 115). Subcutaneous fibromata, neurofibromata of peripheral nerves and viscera are common. Many have skeletal abnormalities and pseudoarthroses.

**Complications**

Phaeochromocytoma and glioma are common. At least 50% develop some neurological impairment.

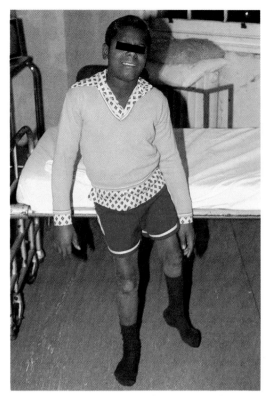

**Fig. 114** Old poliomyelitis with shortening of leg.

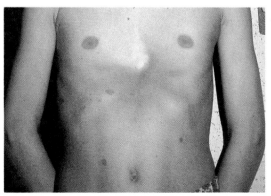

**Fig. 115** Café-au-lait spots and pectus excavatum.

# Neuromuscular and Joint Disorders (6)

## Myasthenia gravis

**Incidence**

Uncommon in early childhood. Peak incidence in adolescent girls.

**Aetiology**

Autoimmune disorder; anticholinesterase antibodies can be demonstrated in majority.

**Clinical features**

Gradual onset of muscle weakness, with early fatigue. Loss of facial expression, arm weakness, chewing difficulty and ptosis (Fig. 116) are common. Transient form of myasthenia gravis occurs in infants of mothers with the disease due to transplacental passage of antibodies.

**Diagnosis**

Clinically confirmed by showing prompt improvement with intravenous edrophonium (Tensilon) (Fig. 117).

**Management**

Long-acting anticholinesterase drugs such as pyridostigmine. Thymectomy often helpful.

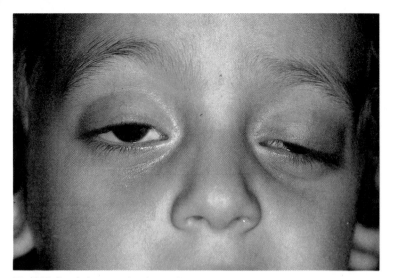

**Fig. 116** Ptosis in myasthenia gravis.

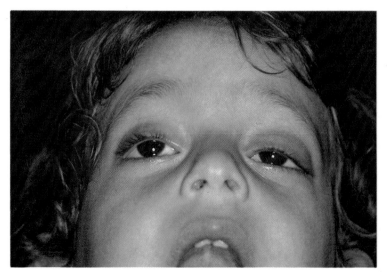

**Fig. 117** Improvement after intravenous edrophonium.

## 9 | Neuromusclar and Joint Disorders (7)

## Arthritis

*Pyogenic arthritis*
Usually a single, hot, swollen, tender joint with painful restriction of movement. *Staphylococcus aureus* is the commonest infective organism. Surgical drainage is often necessary for diagnosis and treatment.

*Rheumatic fever*
There has been a dramatic reduction in the incidence of this disease in developed countries. Classically there is an acute migratory polyarthritis associated with fever, rash and sometimes subcutaneous nodules. Carditis is the most serious long-term complication, resulting in permanent valvular damage.

*Henoch-Schönlein purpura*
A common allergic vasculitis which causes an easily recognisable clinical picture. There is a characteristic purpuric rash (see Figs 67–69), flitting arthritis or arthralgia, abdominal pain and haematuria. The majority resolve rapidly and require only rest and analgesia.

*Juvenile chronic arthritis (JCA)*

Peak incidence of systemic disease is between 1 and 5 years of age. Recurrent painful swelling and stiffness of both small (Fig. 118) and large joints (Figs 119, 120) is common in older children. Weight loss and mild anaemia are associated findings. Joint inflammation can be reduced by appropriate choice of anti-inflammmatory drugs. Exercise, physiotherapy, hydrotherapy and night splints help to limit deformity. Acute inflammatory episodes often remit spontaneously, but sometimes only after many years.

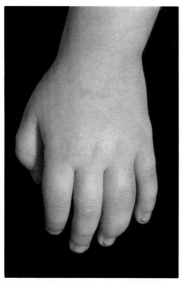

**Fig. 118** Swelling of small joints of the hand in JCA. (By courtesy of Dr B. Ansell.)

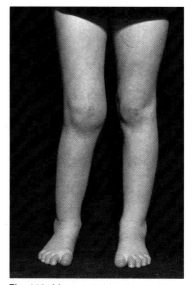

**Fig. 119** Monoarthritis of knee. (By courtesy of Dr B. Ansell.)

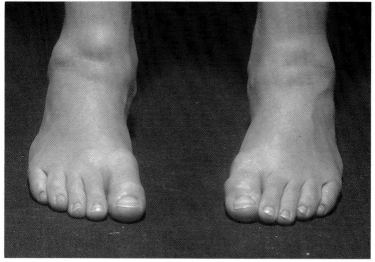

**Fig. 120** Gross swelling of ankles. (By courtesy of Dr B. Ansell.)

# 10 | Malignancy (1)

## Leukaemia

**Incidence**

Commonest childhood malignancy; 85% have acute lymphoblastic leukaemia (ALL).

**Clinical features**

Pallor, lethargy, recurrent infections, fever and spontaneous bruising are common. Hepatosplenomegaly, lymphadenopathy and bone tenderness sometimes occur.

**Diagnosis**

Neonatal leukaemia, though rare, may present with characteristic subcutaneous deposits (Fig. 121). Anaemia, thrombocytopenia and blast cells in peripheral blood. Excessive blast cells in bone marrow confirm the diagnosis.

**Management**

Full discussion of treatment and prognosis with the family is very important. Transfusions of blood, platelets or granulocytes are often necessary. Maintenance chemotherapy with several cytotoxic drugs will continue for several years. Bone marrow transplantation is becoming an important method of treatment.

**Prognosis**

At least 60% 5-year survival now occurs in ALL.

## Histiocytosis

**Pathology**

Abnormal proliferation of histiocytes; variable disease spectrum which sometimes runs malignant course.

**Clinical features**

Clearly defined lytic bone lesions, often involving the skull, are usually benign (eosinophilic granuloma). Systemic disease with fever, hepatosplenomegaly, lymphadenopathy, seborrhoeic rash or skin deposits (Figs 122, 123) is more serious.

**Management**

Systemic disease may respond to cytotoxic chemotherapy similar to treatment for acute leukaemia.

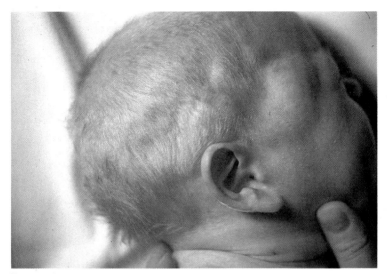

**Fig. 121** Subcutaneous lesions of neonatal leukaemia.

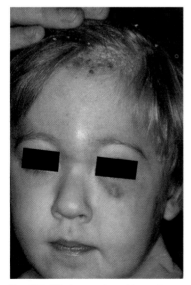

**Fig. 122** Histiocytosis—skin and scalp lesions.

**Fig. 123** Seborrhoeic scalp lesions of histiocytosis.

# Malignancy (2)

## Wilms' tumour (nephroblastoma)

**Clinical features**

Most are found as an asymptomatic abdominal mass (Fig. 124). Haematuria and abdominal pain are sometimes present.

**Diagnosis**

Ultrasound examination of kidney or intravenous urogram show distortion of the pelvicalyceal system.

**Management and prognosis**

Chemotherapy reduces the size of the tumour mass before surgery is performed. Postoperative radiotherapy is sometimes given. Overall 5-year survival is at least 80%. Metastases are often present at the time of diagnosis, but frequently respond to chemotherapy or irradiation.

## Neuroblastoma

**Clinical features**

Usually present as abdominal mass indistinguishable from Wilms' tumour on clinical examination.

**Diagnosis**

Abdominal X-ray may show tumour calcification. Adrenal tumours displace the kidney but do not usually distort the pelvicalyceal system on intravenous urogram or ultrasound examination. Elevated urinary catecholamine levels (VMA and HVA) confirm the diagnosis in 90% cases and are also a sensitive indicator of recurrence. Bony metastases (Fig. 125) sometimes occur.

**Management and prognosis**

Surgical excision followed by radiotherapy. 5-year survival is 60%; occasional spontaneous recovery reported.

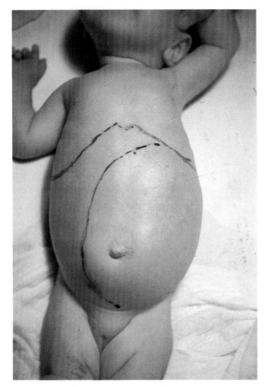

**Fig. 124** Wilms' tumour presenting as abdominal distension.

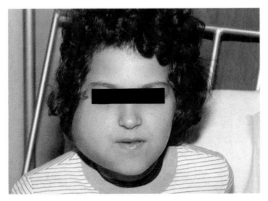

**Fig. 125** Secondary neuroblastoma of mandible.

| # Malignancy (3)

## Cerebral tumour

**Incidence**

Second most common childhood malignancy. Most are located in the posterior fossa.

**Clinical features**

Headache, vomiting, ataxia or visual disturbance are common presenting symptoms. Behavioural disturbance, mood change, convulsions sometimes occur. Cranial nerve palsies (Fig. 126) are often found in brain stem tumours.

**Management and prognosis**

Surgical resection when possible, but this is often difficult or incomplete. Medulloblastomas are often radiosensitive and 5-year survival is now at least 60%. Long-term complications of the tumour or treatment, particularly growth and endocrine disturbance, are almost invariable in surviviors.

## Other malignancy

Solid tumours are uncommon in childhood, but retinoblastoma, rhabdomyosarcoma, osteosarcoma, Hodgkin's disease, and lymphoma (Fig. 127) may occur. Bilateral retinoblastoma has a strong familial incidence, and a good prognosis for survival with early treatment.

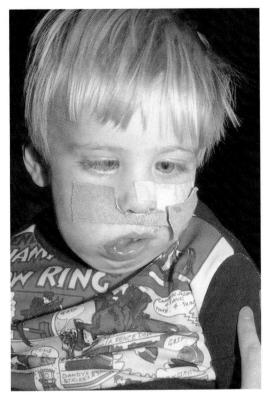

**Fig. 126** VI and VII nerve palsies due to brain stem glioma.

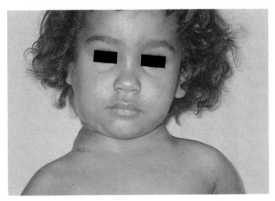

**Fig. 127** Hodgkin's lymphoma.

# Haematological Disorders (1)

## Thalassaemia

**Inheritance**

Autosomal recessive; each pregnancy from parents with thalassaemia minor (heterozygous) carries a 1 in 4 risk of producing homozygous major disease in the infant.

**Aetiology**

Failure of synthesis of $\alpha$ or $\beta$ globin chains.

**Clinical features**

$\alpha$-thalassaemia is commoner in Asians. Homozygous $\alpha$-thalassaemia results in hydrops fetalis with intrauterine or early neonatal death. $\beta$-thalassaemia occurs mainly in Mediterranean populations. When fetal haemoglobin (HbF) levels decline after the first few months, the child develops severe anaemia, hepatosplenomegaly due to extramedullary haemopoiesis, and sometimes cardiac failure. Compensatory bone marrow hyperplasia produces characteristic expansion of the skull and facial bones in older children (Fig. 128). Skull X-rays show the characteristic hair-on-end appearance.

**Management**

Regular blood transfusions are necessary thoughout life.

**Complications**

Frequent transfusions cause chronic iron overload. Continuous subcutaneous infusions of an iron chelating agent (desferrioxamine) may improve survival. Death, usually secondary to cardiomyopathy, occurs in early adult life. Growth and puberty failure, diabetes mellitus, skin pigmentation (Fig. 129) and liver damage are other manifestations of chronic iron overload.

**Antenatal diagnosis**

Affected fetuses may be detected by analysis of globin chain synthesis of fetal blood, or more recently, DNA analysis of chorionic villus biopsy samples.

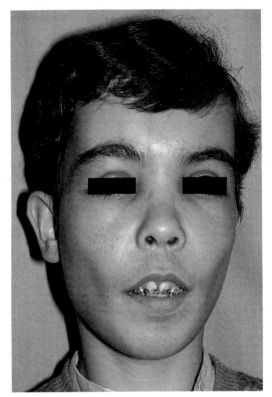

**Fig. 128** Bone hyperplasia in β-thalassaemia intermedia.

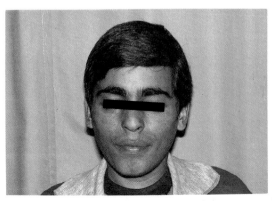

**Fig. 129** Skin pigmentation in thalassaemia.

| # Haematological Disorders (2)

## Sickle cell disease

**Aetiology**

Common; haemoglobinopathy with sickle cell trait found in 15% of blacks; autosomal recessive inheritance.

**Clinical features**

Chronic anaemia, recurrent bone pains with tenderness and swelling, fever and jaundice (Fig. 130). Chronic leg ulcers, haematuria, chest and abdominal pain are common.

**Management**

Symptomatic treatment of painful crises. Prompt antibiotic treatment of infection.

## Idiopathic thrombocytopenic purpura (ITP)

**Aetiology**

Often occurs after viral infections, especially rubella. Platelet antibodies usually detectable.

**Clinical features and diagnosis**

Spontaneous petechiae and superficial bruising (Fig. 131). Other, more serious causes of thrombocytopenia must be excluded.

**Course and prognosis**

Majority recover spontaneously within a few months; occasionally chronic, requiring splenectomy.

## Bleeding disorders

**Aetiology**

Haemophilia A (factor VIII deficiency) is the most common.

**Clinical features**

Spontaneous bruising or excessive bleeding after minimal trauma producing haemarthrosis (Fig. 132), deep haematomas or mucosal haemorrhage.

**Management**

All trauma and surgical procedures must be treated with intravenous factor concentrates. Chronic joint damage can be reduced with early treatment of trauma and bleeding.

**Antenatal diagnosis**

Factor assay of fetal blood sample.

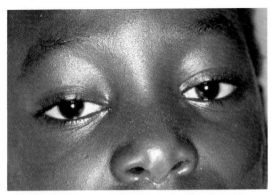

**Fig. 130** Jaundiced sclera in sickle cell anaemia.

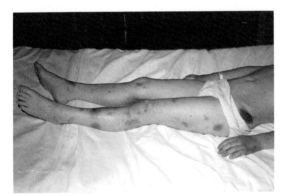

**Fog.131** Bruising in ITP.

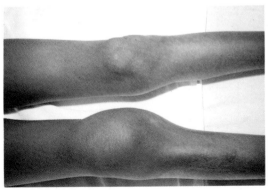

**Fig. 132** Haemarthrosis in haemophilia. (By courtesy of Dr A. Kilby.)

# Surgery, Orthopaedics and Trauma (1)

## Bat ears

**Inheritance**

Often autosomal dominant.

**Clinical features**

Large protruding ears, usually bilateral (Fig. 133).

**Pathology**

Defect in the normal folding process of the anti-helix.

**Significance and treatment**

Corrective surgery when protrusion of ears is cosmetically unacceptable.

## Torticollis

**Aetiology**

Usually acute onset of unknown aetiology. Chronic painless torticollis may be secondary to sternomastoid fibrosis, intrauterine posture, cervical hemivertebrae, or ocular imbalance.

**Clinical features**

In acute painful torticollis or the common wryneck (Fig. 134) there is a sudden onset of limitation of neck rotation with an intensely painful sternomastoid muscle. The head is sometimes tilted towards the affected side.

**Management**

Spontaneous recovery occurs within days in acute torticollis or months in postural torticollis. Gentle physiotherapy may be helpful.

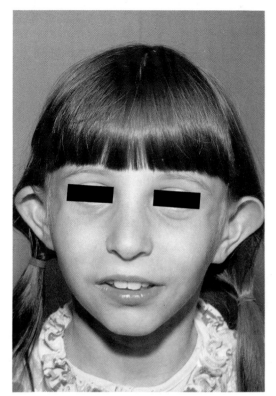

**Fig. 133** Bat ears.

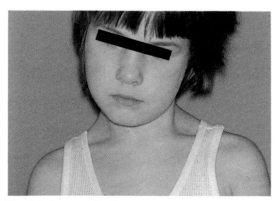

**Fig. 134** Acute torticollis.

# Surgery, Orthopaedics and Trauma (2)

## Cleft lip and palate

**Management**

Cleft lip (Fig. 135) is repaired as early as possible and the palate within the first year of life. Further plastic surgery to elevate the ala nasae to improve the cosmetic appearance is sometimes necessary in later childhood (Fig. 136). Additional specialist help may be required to deal with orthodontic problems, speech difficulties and Eustachian tube obstruction.

## Choanal atresia

**Incidence**

Rare anomaly in which there is absence or narrowing of the posterior nares.

**Clinical features**

Bilateral choanal atresia causes cyanosis and respiratory obstruction in the newborn. In unilateral choanal atresia, the condition causes unilateral rhinorrhoea and diagnosis is often not made until later in childhood.

**Management**

Urgent provision of an oral airway is needed in bilateral choanal atresia. The membranous posterior nares are then surgically excised and a small tube left in situ until the new orifice has epithelialised (Fig. 137).

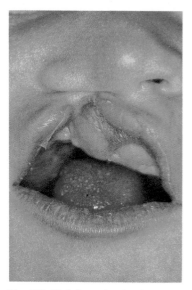

**Fig. 135** Cleft lip and palate in infancy.

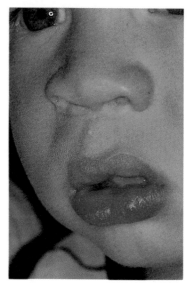

**Fig. 136** Repaired cleft lip.

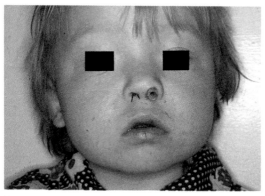

**Fig. 137** Choanal atresia with tube in nostril.

# Surgery, Orthopaedics and Trauma (3)

## Developmental limb anomalies

**Incidence**

Common, particularly anomalies of the hand and arms.

**Aetiology**

Usually unknown. Absent radius or limb reduction defects may occur after a major vascular catastrophe in fetal life. Phocomelia is known to occur with maternal ingestion of drugs such as thalidomide in early pregnancy.

**Clinical features**

Extra digits (polydactyly) of the hands and feet (Fig. 138) are extremely common and are often of autosomal dominant inheritance. Extra digits on the hand usually require surgical excision in early life. Polydactyly of the toes may require excision when the provision of comfortable footwear is difficult when the child is older.

Syndactyly (Fig. 139) particularly of the 2nd and 3rd toes is extremely common and is never of any functional significance.

Absent radius and thumb (Fig. 140) is sometimes found in association with thrombocytopenia or anaemia.

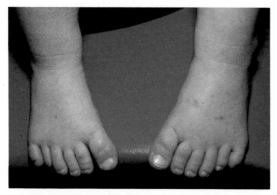

**Fig. 138** Polydactyly of toes.

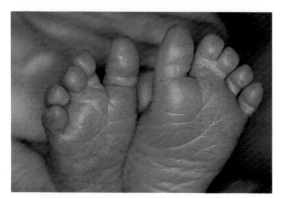

**Fig. 139** Syndactyly of 2nd and 3rd toes.

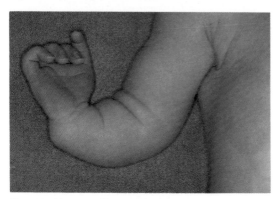

**Fig. 140** Absent radius and thumb.

# Surgery, Orthopaedics and Trauma (4)

## Development limb anomalies (cont)

Missing digits (Fig. 141) sometimes occur.

Complete absence of the hand (Fig. 142) is the most common limb reduction deformity. Prosthetic substitutes should be provided before the age of acquisition of skills requiring hand co-ordination.

Claw hand (Fig. 143) and foot are uncommon anomalies of major functional significance. Surgery is usually considered, but is not always necessary.

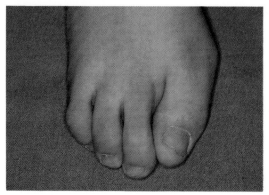

**Fig. 141** Missing digit.

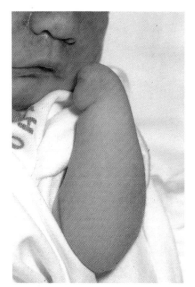

**Fig. 142** Limb reduction deformity with absent hand.

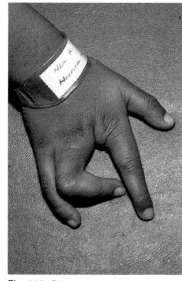

**Fig. 143** Claw hand.

# Surgery, Orthopaedics and Trauma (5)

## Postural deformities of the leg and foot

*Bow legs*
In the first 2 years of life the tibia of the normal child has an outward curve and internal rotation. This bow-legged appearance (Fig. 144) is often more apparent when walking begins. Spontaneous improvement occurs.

*Knock-knees*
After 2 years of age, there may be unequal growth of the femoral condyles which gives rise to the knock-knee posture (genu valgum) (Fig. 145). Girls are more commonly affected.

Gradual improvement occurs and by 6–7 years of age the legs are usually straight.

*In-toeing*
The most common cause is metatarsus varus. The feet tend to curve medially because of adduction of the forefoot (Fig. 146). The natural tendency is for improvement with growth, although surgery is occasionally necessary. Excessive internal rotation of the femora is common in girls and this also causes in-toeing. Treatment is unnecessary because spontaneous resolution occurs.

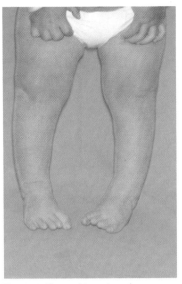

**Fig. 144** Normal bow legs in infancy.

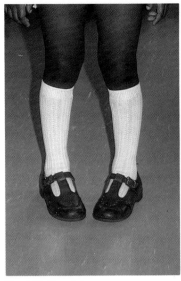

**Fig. 145** Knock-knee.

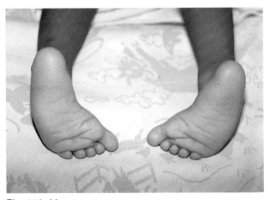

**Fig. 146** Metatarsus varus.

# Surgery, Orthopaedics and Trauma (6)

## Scoliosis

**Aetiology**

Usually idiopathic; occurs mainly in adolescent girls.

**Clinical features**

Spinal curvature is best detected by asking the child to bend forwards with the arms hanging freely. Usually asymptomatic, but can progress to severe cosmetic deformity. Severe scoliosis may cause respiratory embarrassment or spinal cord complications. Midline lesions, such as haemangiomas (Fig. 147), hairy naevi, or lipomas, may indicate an underlying vertebral anomaly, particularly when they occur in the lumbosacral region.

**Management**

Bracing or surgical correction may be necessary when deformity progresses.

## Hip disorders

**Incidence and aetiology**

The most common cause of limp or hip pain is transient synovitis (irritable hip), or trauma. Avascular necrosis of the femoral head (Perthes' disease) occurs in boys aged 5–10 years. Aetiology is unknown. Obese teenage boys occasionally develop slipped upper femoral epiphyses.

**Clinical features**

Usually sudden onset of limp and hip pain. There is restriction of abduction, extension and internal rotation.

**Diagnosis and management**

X-rays are diagnostic in Perthes' disease (Fig. 148) and slipped femoral epiphyses. Irritable hip is diagnosed after exclusion of infection and specific joint and bone disorders. Irritable hip recovers with a few days or weeks of bed-rest. Limb traction, surgery or internal fixation may be necessary in Perthes' disease and slipped femoral epiphyses.

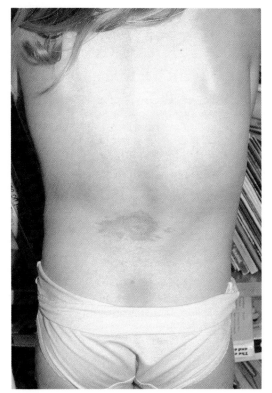

**Fig. 147** Scoliosis and midline haemangioma.

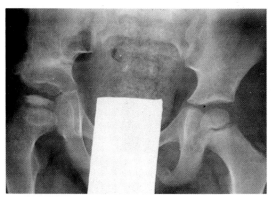

**Fig. 148** X-ray of Perthes' disease.

# Surgery, Orthopaedics and Trauma (7)

## Cystic hygroma

**Clinical features**

Most become apparent in the first year of life. The hygroma is a developmental anomaly of the lymphatic channels which gives rise to an ill-defined fluctuant cystic mass (Fig. 149), usually in the neck.

**Management**

Surgical excision is necessary as the mass slowly enlarges, causing cosmetic embarrassment, and occasionally becomes infected or causes respiratory distress.

## Lipoma

**Incidence**

Common.

**Clinical features**

Soft subcutaneous mass (Fig. 150) which may be located anywhere on the body. Can usually be distinguished from lymphangiomas, which transilluminate.

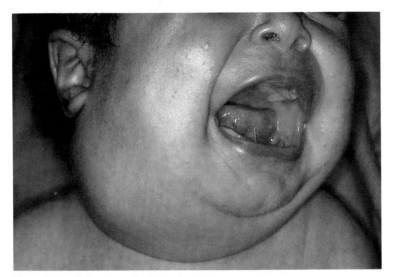

**Fig. 149** Cystic hygroma in the neck.

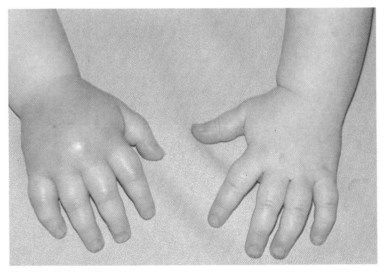

**Fig. 150** Lipoma of hand.

# Surgery, Orthopaedics and Trauma (8)

## Fractures

**Clinical features**

Pain, swelling and loss of function of a limb. A history of trauma is not always obtained, particularly in the very young.

**Management**

Exact anatomical reposition is not always necessary in children, as efficient remodelling ensures a good end result. Fracture of the humerus in young infants (usually due to birth trauma) requires only a collar-and-cuff sling. Callus formation and healing is more rapid in young children. Even a major fracture of the femur will heal rapidly after a few weeks of immobilisation in gallows traction (Fig. 151).

**Complications**

Arterial ischaemia (Fig. 153) or nerve injury are the major complications of any fracture.

## Osteogenesis imperfecta

**Clinical features**

The severe congenital form is usually lethal in utero or shortly after birth. In the later onset type of osteogenesis imperfecta, fractures occur spontaneously or with minimal trauma.

**Complications**

Severe chest and limb deformity (Fig. 152) may result if fractures are not recognised and treated appropriately. Although the frequency of fractures decreases with age, the child usually has short stature and some permanent deformity and disability in later life. Progressive deafness may also occur.

**Fig. 151** Gallow's traction. Legs in traction, but still partly mobile!

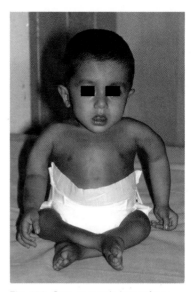

**Fig. 152** Osteogenesis imperfecta with bony deformity.

**Fig. 153** Volkmann's ischaemic contracture of forearm secondary to supracondylar fracture of humerus. (By courtesy of Dr A. Kilby.)

# Surgery, Orthopaedics and Trauma (9)

## Burns and scalds

**Clinical features**

The most common scald happens to the toddler who pulls boiling water onto his face, neck, shoulder and upper arm (Fig. 154). Flame burns tend to happen to older children. When clothes catch fire, burns may involve extensive areas of the body (Fig. 155) and are often deep.

**Management**

Treatment depends on the extent and severity of the burn. Emergency measures consist of pain relief (particularly for superficial scalds), ensuring an adequate airway, and resuscitation with plasma volume expanders when there are signs of shock. If burns involve more than 10% of the child's surface area, intravenous therapy will be necessary. Large quantities of fluid, blood and protein are lost from burned areas. Tetanus toxoid should always be given. Infection should be prevented by barrier nursing of exposed burns or by the closed method with topical antibiotics such as silver sulphadiazine under occlusive dressings (Fig. 156). Systemic antibiotics are given if there are specific indications.

**Course and prognosis**

Superficial burns quickly form a protective eschar when left exposed. This eschar gradually lifts off when new epithelium has formed (Fig. 157). Skin grafts may be necessary for deep burns, extensive burns or to relieve tight contractures.

**Prevention**

Burns should be preventable by education of the public, and safeguards in design of heating appliances and children's clothing.

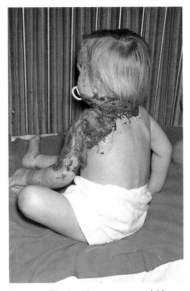

**Fig. 154** Typical hot water scald in toddler.

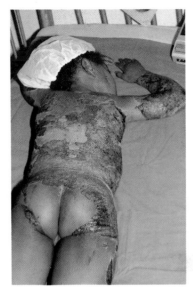

**Fig. 155** Extensive flame burns.

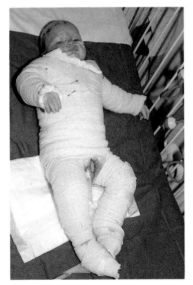

**Fig. 156** Extensive burns treated by closed dressings.

**Fig. 157** New epithelium forming after a scald.

# 13 | Non-accidental Injury

**Aetiology**

Non-accidental injury (NAI) or child abuse usually occurs when parents or child-carers injure their dependent but demanding child. Child abuse may also take the more subtle form of neglect or deprivation.

**Clinical features**

There is often a history of supposed accident. Suspicion should be aroused when history and injury are conflicting, inconsistent or repeated. Unexplained fractures or bruises, particularly multiple or of varying age, are often found. Rough handling or direct hitting may cause fractures of ribs or long bones. Gripping and shaking an infant may leave finger-mark bruises. Cigarette burns (Fig. 158) leave discrete punched out lesions. Whip marks (Fig. 159) are more common in older children. Dip-burns to the buttocks and feet (Fig. 160) occur when an infant is lowered into scalding water. Human bite marks (Fig. 161) are sometimes clearly seen.

**Management**

If non-accidental injury is suspected, society has a responsibility to protect the child. In addition to medical treatment of the injuries, this will involve assessment of the family situation and possible contributing factors, and exclusion of alternative diagnoses. With careful supervision and sympathetic support, many children can continue to be cared for by their parents. Occasionally the child may be safer in the care of others.

PAEDIATRICS

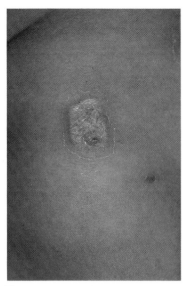

**Fig. 158** Cigarette burn.

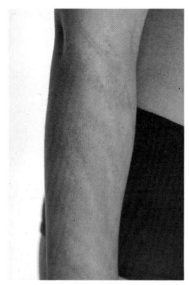

**Fig. 159** Whip marks.

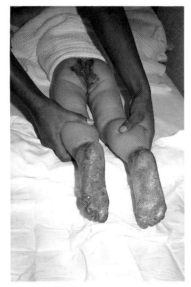

**Fig. 160** Dip-burns.

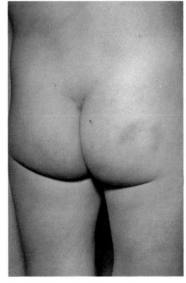

**Fig. 161** Human bite marks.

## Congenital anomalies

*Congenital ptosis*
Often familial and usually unilateral (Fig. 162). In the majority of cases binocular vision is unaffected. Shortening of the levator palpebrae superioris may improve the cosmetic appearance or improve vision if ptosis is severe.

*Microphthalmos*
Developmental anomaly often associated with congenital rubella. If the palpebral fissure is short (Fig. 163), surgery may improve the cosmetic appearance.

*Coloboma*
Developmental anomaly of the iris (Fig. 164). Often familial. Vision usually unaffected. Occasionally associated with a retinal anomaly.

*External angular dermoid*
Commonly found around the orbit, usually above and lateral to the palpebral fissure (see Fig. 71). Surgery usually necessary to improve appearance, because the cysts gradually increase in size.

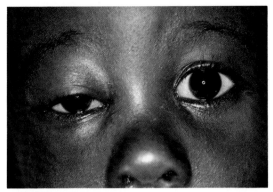

**Fig. 162** Congenital ptosis.

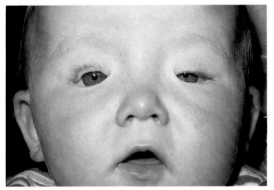

**Fig. 163** Microphthalmos and ptosis.

**Fig. 164** Coloboma.

**Eye Disorders (2)**

## Strabismus (squint)

**Incidence**

Common in early childhood. All fixed squints and any squint that persists after 5–6 months of age require careful evaluation.

**Aetiology**

Usually due to failure of development of binocular co-ordination of unknown aetiology.

**Clinical features**

The diagnosis is usually obvious on clinical examination (Fig. 165). Symmetrical corneal reflection or occlusion testing may assist diagnosis in less obvious cases. Epicanthic folds may give rise to a false appearance of squint.

**Management and prognosis**

Suppression of vision (amblyopia) in the deviated eye may be permanent if squint is not detected and treated early. Correction of refractive error and occlusion of the non-squinting eye are mandatory. Surgery is sometimes necessary.

## Infection and trauma

*Infection*
Conjunctivitis is common in the neonatal period. Recurrent mild conjunctivitis (Fig. 166) is usually due to non-patency of the nasolacrimal duct which resolves towards the end of the first year of life.

*Trauma*
Painful corneal abrasions are usually caused by foreign bodies in the eye. Lacerations of the eyelid (Fig. 167) and penetrating eye injuries are usually the result of direct trauma.

**Fig. 165** Squint.

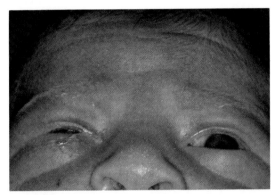

**Fig. 166** Recurrent minor conjunctivitis.

**Fig. 167** Traumatic eye lesion with laceration and conjunctival haemorrhage.

| # Eye Disorders (3)

## Cataract

**Aetiology**

Usually congenital and sometimes familial. Secondary cataracts occur in rubella embryopathy, galactosaemia and diabetes.

**Clinical features**

An opacity is seen in the lens (Fig. 168). Other ocular anomalies such as nystagmus or visual disturbance are often present.

**Management**

Depends on cause and interference with vision. Early surgery within the first month diminishes the risk of subsequent amblyopia.

## Malignancy

**Aetiology**

Retinoblastoma is the commonest malignant intraocular tumour in childhood. Sometimes has autosomal dominant inheritance.

**Clinical features**

Opacity of the pupil, squint or poor vision in the affected eye. Proptosis (Fig. 169) occurs with tumours involving the orbit, particularly metastatic neuroblastoma.

**Management**

Local treatment of retinoblastoma may include surgery, radiotherapy and cryotherapy. Metastases are rare and long-term prognosis is good.

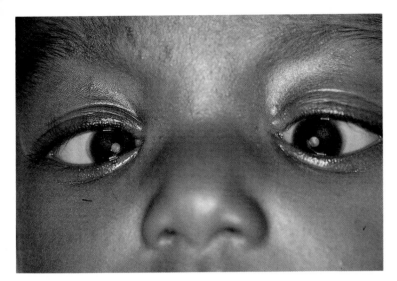

**Fig. 168** Bilateral cataracts.

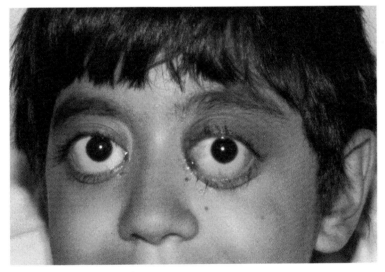

**Fig. 169** Bilateral proptosis.

# Syndromes (1)

## Down's syndrome

**Synonym**

Trisomy 21; used to be called 'mongolism'.

**Incidence**

1 in 600 live births; majority due to trisomy 21, 3% due to translocation. Increased risk of trisomy 21 with increased maternal age.

**Clinical features**

Characteristic facial appearance (Fig. 170), hypotonia, low birth weight and growth retardation. Prominent epicanthic folds, Brushfield's spots and single transverse palmar creases (simian crease) are often present but also occur in 18% of normal children.

**Course and prognosis**

Mental retardation always occurs, but varies in severity. There is a high mortality in the first year due to congenital heart disease and respiratory infection.

## Turner's syndrome

**Incidence**

Monosomic X syndrome with ovarian dysgenesis occurs in 1 in 5000 live births.

**Clinical features**

Short stature, webbing of the neck and failure of secondary sexual development (Fig. 171). Coarctation of the aorta occurs in girls and pulmonary stenosis is often found in boys with similar physical characteristics (Noonan's syndrome).

**Management**

Cyclical oestrogen replacement will promote secondary sexual development in adolescence, but infertility is invariable.

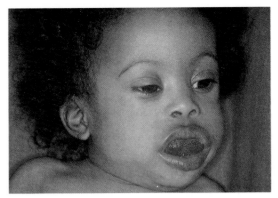

**Fig. 170** Typical facies of Down's syndrome.

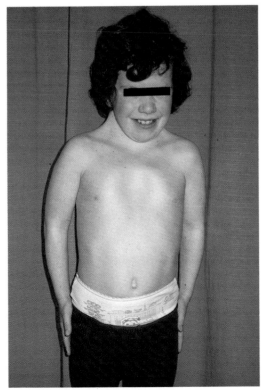

**Fig. 171** Turner's syndrome.

| **Syndromes (2)**

## Sturge-Weber syndrome

**Inheritance**

Majority sporadic; occasionally autosomal dominant inheritance.

**Clinical features**

Facial port-wine stain, characteristically in the trigeminal distribution (Fig. 172), seizures and sometimes mental retardation. A meningeal haemangioma is often present on the same side and may cause a contralateral hemiplegia, cerebral atrophy, cerebral calcification and macrocephaly.

## Klippel-Trenaunay-Weber syndrome

**Inheritance**

Sporadic occurrence.

**Clinical features**

Cutaneous haemangiomata and asymmetric limb hypertrophy (Fig. 173). Associated arteriovenous fistulae are common and lymphangiomatous anomalies sometimes occur.

**Management**

Surgery may be necessary when there is disproportionate limb growth or troublesome arteriovenous fistulae.

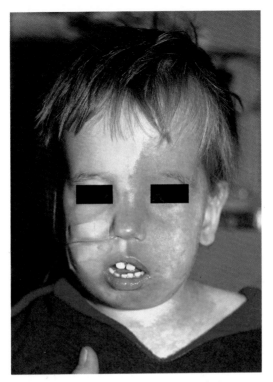

**Fig. 172** Facial haemangioma in Sturge-Weber syndrome.

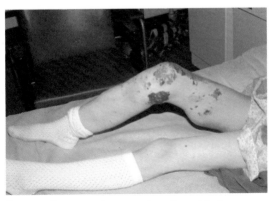

**Fig. 173** Cutaneous haemangiomata and limb hypertrophy in Klippel-Trenaunay-Weber syndrome.

# Syndromes (3)

## Tuberose sclerosis

**Synonym**

Epiloia.

**Inheritance**

Autosomal dominant but at least 80% are due to fresh mutation.

**Clinical features**

Severity and expression of the syndrome varies enormously, even within families. Usually epilepsy, mental deficiency and some skin manifestations occur. All have granulomatous lesions (tubers) in the brain which become visible on CT scan by 7 or 8 years of age. Skin manifestations include the typical adenoma sebaceum (a papular rash on the cheeks) (Fig. 174), fibromas, shagreen patch, café-au-lait spots, and depigmented patches (Fig. 175). Visceral hamartomas and retinal lesions are common.

## Waardenburg's syndrome

**Inheritance**

Autosomal dominant.

**Clinical features**

White forelock (Fig. 176) or partial albinism and congenital deafness are usual. Sometimes there is heterochromia of the iris and vitiligo of the skin (Fig. 177).

**Management**

Deafness is the most serious feature; usually bilateral and severe sensorineural deafness.

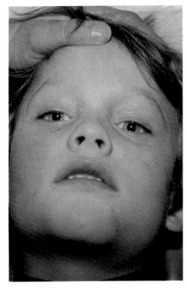

**Fig. 174** Adenoma sebaceum.

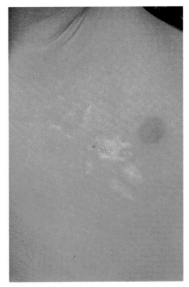

**Fig. 175** Depigmented patches in tuberose sclerosis.

**Fig. 176** White forelock of Waardenburg's syndrome.

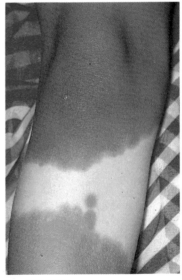

**Fig. 177** Vitiligo.

## Mucopolysaccharidoses

**Inheritance**  Autosomal recessive.

**Aetiology**  Various specific enzyme deficiencies which result in accumulation of cytoplasmic mucopolysaccharides. Most common types are Hurler's (type I), Hunter's (type II), Morquio's (type IV) and Sanfilippo's (type VII) syndromes.

**Clinical features**  The infant appears normal at birth. Coarse facies (Fig. 178), growth retardation, mental retardation, skeletal abnormalities (Fig. 179) and hepatosplenomegaly gradually progress and become obvious within the first 2 years of life. Cloudy cornea is found in Hurler's syndrome. In Morquio's syndrome, there is severe skeletal deformity (Fig. 180) and growth retardation, but normal intelligence.

**Management**  There is no cure, but bone marrow transplantation may be a useful form of treatment to halt the progression of the condition, and may cause it to regress.

## Short-limbed dwarfism

**Incidence**  Achondroplasia, the most common chondrodysplasia, occurs in about 1 in 10 000 live births.

**Inheritance**  Autosomal dominant, but the majority are fresh mutations.

**Clinical features**  Short stature, short limbs and macrocephaly always occur (Fig. 181). Specific diagnosis is usually made on radiological examination.

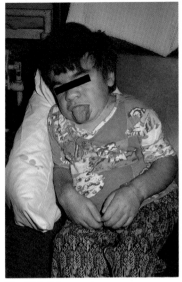

**Fig. 178** Advanced mucopolysaccharidosis.

**Fig. 179** Hurler's syndrome.

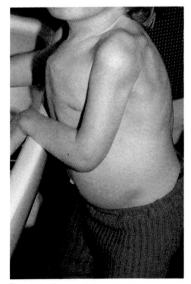

**Fig. 180** Chest deformity in Morquio's syndrome.

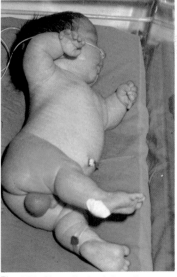

**Fig. 181** Short-limbed dwarfism.

# Syndromes (5)

## De Lange syndrome

**Inheritance**

Sporadic condition of unknown aetiology.

**Clinical features**

Short stature, failure to thrive, and hirsutism (Fig. 182) are invariable. Bushy eyebrows, long curling eyelashes, micrognathia, small nose with anteverted nostrils, and down-turned mouth (Fig. 183) give a characteristic facial appearance.

**Course and prognosis**

All are severely mentally retarded and death usually occurs in early childhood.

## Crouzon's syndrome

**Inheritance**

Autosomal dominant with variable expression.

**Clinical features**

Cranial facial dysostosis with craniosynostosis of coronal, lambdoid and sagittal sutures. Ocular proptosis because of shallow orbits and hypertelorism give a characteristic facial appearance (Fig. 184).

**Management**

Surgery to allow normal brain growth when craniosynostosis is severe, or for cosmetic reasons.

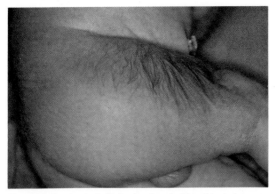

**Fig. 182** Particularly hairy leg in a baby with de Lange syndrome.

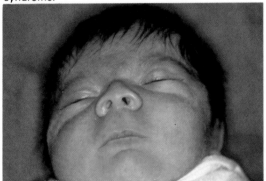

**Fig. 183** Characteristic facial appearance in de Lange syndrome.

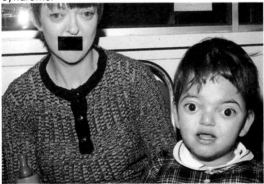

**Fig. 184** Crouzon's syndrome. (By courtesy of Dr A. Kilby.)

| # Syndromes (6)

## Progeria

Incidence
: Extremely rare syndrome of unknown aetiology.

Inheritance
: Most cases are sporadic.

Clinical features
: Premature and rapid ageing with onset in infancy. Severe growth retardation, loss of subcutaneous fat and generalised atherosclerosis (Fig. 185). Alopecia, hypoplastic nails and flexion deformities sometimes occur.

Course and prognosis
: There is normal brain development and intelligence. Life expectancy is severely shortened (average 15 years) and death is usually due to myocardial infarction.

## Russell-Silver syndrome

Incidence
: Uncommon.

Inheritance
: Usually sporadic.

Clinical features
: A syndrome of extreme growth retardation of prenatal onset, asymmetry of the limbs and shortened incurved fifth finger. There is craniofacial dysostosis with small triangular facies and a small down-turned mouth (Fig. 186).

Course and prognosis
: Gradual improvement in growth rate may occur in later childhood, but final adult height remains small.

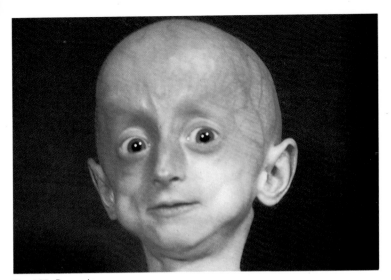

**Fig. 185** Progeria.

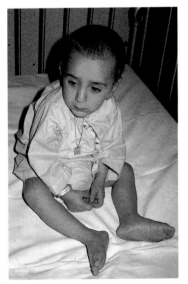

**Fig. 186** Russell-Silver dwarfism.

## Lesch-Nyhan syndrome

**Inheritance**  X-linked.

**Aetiology**  Enzyme deficiency resulting in over-production of uric acid; antenatal diagnosis now available for high-risk families.

**Clinical features**  Mental retardation, athetoid or choreiform movements, dysarthria, muscle weakness, brisk tendon reflexes and extensor plantar responses. Characteristic self-mutilation (Fig. 187) due to uncontrollable aggressive impulses which appear to be unrelated to impaired sensation or hyperuricaemia.

**Management**  Hyperuricaemia can be controlled with allopurinol, but clinical course remains unchanged.

## Lowe's syndrome

**Synonym**  Oculocerebrorenal syndrome.

**Inheritance**  X-linked.

**Clinical features**  Mental retardation, hypotonia, joint hypermobility, hyperactivity and growth retardation are common (Fig. 189). Cataracts and blindness usually occur. Renal tubular dysfunction and cryptorchidism are also found.

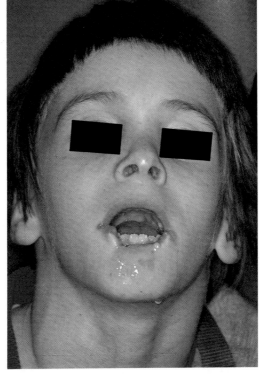

**Fig. 187** Lesch-Nyhan syndrome showing effects of self-mutilation.

**Fig. 188** A mentally handicapped blind child with Lowe's syndrome.

| **Syndromes (8)**

## Branchial arch syndrome

**Synonym**

Facioauriculovertebral syndrome.

**Incidence**

Relatively common. Often associated with ocular or vertebral anomalies or epibulbar dermoids (Goldenhar syndrome).

**Clinical features**

Hypoplastic pinna with absent external auditory meatus (Fig. 189). Usually unilateral. Accessory pre-auricular tags are common. Unilateral hearing loss common, but speech is usually normal if hearing is normal on the other side. Facial hypoplasia, and branchial cleft remnants in the anterolateral neck are common.

**Management**

Early assessment of hearing is important. Cosmetic surgery is usually desirable but not always satisfactory.

## Ectodermal dysplasia

**Incidence and Inheritance**

Rare; X-linked and autosomal dominant inheritance described.

**Clinical features**

Hypoplastic or absent nails and teeth (Fig. 190). Hair is usually fine and sparse. Abnormalities of sweat and sebaceous glands also occur in some varieties.

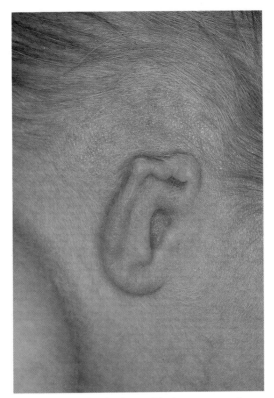

**Fig. 189** Hypoplastic pinna with absent external auditory meatus.

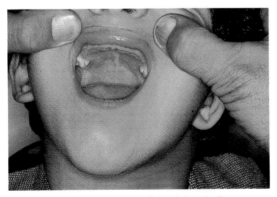

**Fig. 190** Absent teeth in ectodermal dysplasia.

# Syndromes (9)

## Menkes' syndrome (Menkes' kinky hair syndrome)

**Incidence**

Rare.

**Inheritance**

X-linked recessive.

**Aetiology**

Probably a defect of copper-binding protein metalloprotein.

**Clinical features**

Characteristic sparse, twisted 'kinky' hair (Figs 191, 192) which has partial breakages and twists on microscopic examination. There is profound progressive neurological deterioration and failure to thrive from early infancy. Death is usual in the first few years.

**Antenatal diagnosis**

Excessive copper uptake in cultured amniotic cells has been demonstrated.

## Cockayne's syndrome

**Incidence**

Rare.

**Inheritance**

Autosomal recessive; antenatal disgnosis now possible.

**Clinical features**

Short stature with loss of subcutaneous fat from infancy. Dorsal kyphosis (Fig. 193), limitation of joint movement, grey sparse hair and mental retardation are present. Retinal pigmentation and photosensitive skin are common.

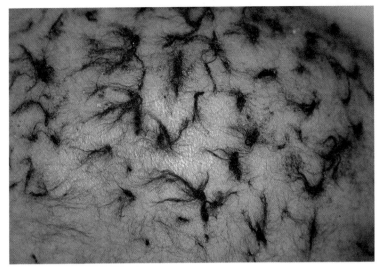

**Fig. 191** Kinky hair in Menkes' syndrome.

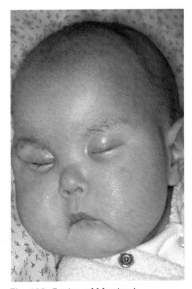

**Fig. 192** Facies of Menkes' syndrome showing puffy cheeks and kinky eyebrows.

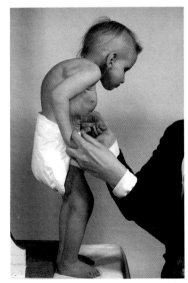

**Fig. 193** Cockayne's syndrome.

## Vision

Myelination of the optic pathways is incomplete at term; early correction of congenital cataracts or severe ptosis is important for normal visual development. At birth the child will fix for a short while on his mother's face and by 6–8 weeks follows objects in his direct line of vision. From 9 months, small graded white balls (Stycar test balls) can be used to test visual acuity. After 3 years of age, the child can usually match letters with graded letter cards (Fig. 194).

## Hearing

The newborn infant will quieten with soothing noises and within a few weeks of birth reacts to loud noises by startling, or crying. By 6–9 months of age, he will turn his head or move his eyes towards a sound stimulus such as a high pitched rattle or bell at ear level (Fig. 195).
Comprehension and imitation of normal speech indicates that severe hearing loss is unlikely.

**Fig. 194** Testing vision with graded letter cards in a 3-year-old child.

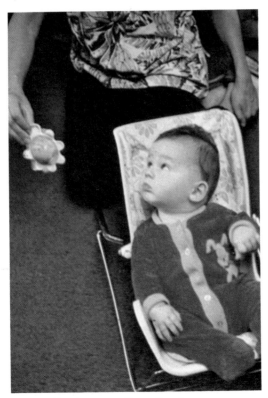

**Fig. 195** Hearing test at 6 months of age.

# Assessment (2)

## Drawings

The pictures a child is asked to draw can provide useful clinical information. He can be asked to 'draw a man' and the parts of the body that he includes in the picture are a good indication of his stage of development. Some pictures may indicate emotional problems that cannot otherwise be communicated to the clinician (Figs 196–199). Sometimes the drawing may reveal an undiscovered clinical feature such as hemianopia in a child who only draws on one side of the paper.

**Fig. 196** A picture of a slim woman by a very obese girl.

**Fig. 197** 'My house' by a child who lived in very poor accommodation.

**Fig. 198** 'A man' by a child who had had a hernia operation. A lump and would with stitches are clearly shown, although on different parts of the body from the operation.

**Fig. 199** 'A man' by a child with food intolerance.

# 17 | Children in Hospital

Admission to hospital is distressing for all of us, but it is worse for children. A child under 5 may not only be frightened by the illness and painful procedures like intravenous infusions and blood tests, but can be even more upset by separation from the family. It is very important that someone already known to the child should stay with him in hospital; preferably this should be the mother or father (Fig. 200). They can often do some of the nursing care; they may feed and comfort a small child, and can also do more complicated things like tube feeding, watching intravenous infusions, and care of a tracheostomy. Parents, siblings and other relatives on the ward often add to the work of the staff because they naturally expect to ask questions about tests and treatment they see. Even so, their presence helps all the staff to care for the ill child better, and makes the stay in hospital much less frightening. A controlled trial has shown that after-effects, such as nightmares, clinging, and a recurrence of enuresis were less common in children whose mothers stayed with them in hospital. A playgroup (Fig. 201) and a school are essential on a children's ward. Play (Fig. 202) allows the children to bear the strain of the admission and often reveals information about their physical and emotional problems. It is very important that a long illness should not interrupt school work.

**Fig. 200** Mother and child in hospital.

**Fig. 201** Hospital playgroup with children and parents.

**Fig. 202** Children at play during hospital admission.

1793   164
21/10/86